Folklore Matters

Folklore Matters

Alan Dundes

The University of Tennessee Press

KNOXVILLE

Cloth: 1st printing, 1989.
Paper: 1st printing, 1992; 2nd printing, 1996.

The paper in this book meets the minimum requirements of the
American National Standard for Permanence of Paper for Printed Library
Materials. ⊗   The binding materials have been chosen for strength
and durability.

Library of Congress Cataloging in Publication Data

Dundes, Alan.
    Folklore matters / Alan Dundes.
        p.   cm.
    Includes bibliographies and index.
    ISBN 0–87049–608–5 (cloth: alk. paper)
    ISBN 0–87049–776–6 (pbk.: alk paper)
      1. Folklore. I. Title.
GR71.D86   1989
398—dc19   88–32616 CIP

Contents

Preface   vii

Acknowledgments   xi

Defining Identity through Folklore   1

The Fabrication of Fakelore   40

The Anthropologist and the
Comparative Method in Folklore   57

Pecking Chickens: A Folk Toy as a
Source for the Study of Worldview   83

On Whether Weather "Proverbs"
Are Proverbs   92

April Fool and April Fish:
Towards a Theory of Ritual Pranks   98

The Psychoanalytic Study
of the Grimms' Tales:
"The Maiden Without Hands" (AT 706)   112

The Building of Skadar:
The Measure of Meaning
of a Ballad of the Balkans   151

Index   169

Preface

Most of my adult life as a professional folklorist has been devoted to explaining to undergraduates, graduate students, and interested members of the general public what folklore is, how we study it, and why folklore matters. Although nearly everyone already possesses personal familiarity with literally hundreds of individual items of folklore, few are aware of the international discipline of folkloristics. Even my many colleagues in other departments of my own and other universities are not really sure what it is that folklorists do. There is a vague sense that folklorists wander out in the field with their tape recorders and their notebooks, jotting down quaint turns of phrase or documenting some archaic village festival. But not many academics are aware that folkloristics is a separate and distinct discipline, straddling the humanities and the social sciences, with its own set of periodicals, bibliographies, methods, and theories. Occasionally a historian or anthropologist or student of literature will stumble upon a sample of folklore research deemed relevant to ongoing historical, anthropological, or literary projects, but, sad to say, the majority of individuals both inside and outside of the academy have only the sketchiest notion of what folklore is all about.

No one book of essays could possibly cover the enormous field of folklore satisfactorily, and this volume is no exception. However, in the eight essays presented, I hope that I can at least give one person's view of the field. In the initial essay, "Defining Identity Through Folklore," I try to demonstrate just how crucial folklore is for establishing a sense of identity or senses of identities.

The next essay seeks to illustrate how feelings of national inferiority can lead well-intentioned scholars to fabricate or alter folklore, thereby producing something spurious which we folklorists call "fakelore."

The third essay takes up the comparative method which by all odds remains as the single most important technique employed by folklorists. Even if one should be primarily interested in structural or psychoanalytic approaches to folklore, as I, for one, am, the critical importance of assembling cognate versions of a given item of folklore is indispensable for these or any other approaches advocated.

The fourth essay briefly puts into practice an abbreviated comparative method in considering a widespread folk toy, namely, the pecking chickens. The intent is to demonstrate how even the seemingly most trivial folkloristic item can, upon analysis, reveal fascinating insights about people and their cultures.

Folklorists spend a good deal of time defining and debating genre theory. The study of folklore is largely the study of particular folklore genres: myth, folktale, legend, ballad, proverb, riddle, superstition, etc. Some genres are admittedly minor, e.g., flyleaf inscriptions; while others are undoubtedly major, e.g., epics. But all genres, major or minor, are worthy of serious study. In the fifth essay, I attempt to delineate what I feel are significant differences between the genres of proverb and superstition.

The sixth essay takes up a neglected folklore genre: the prank. The prank or practical joke is fairly widespread, but it has tended to be ignored by most folklorists. My aim in the essay is to explain why it is appropriate for pranks to be associated with the first of April.

My own bias in folkloristics is decidedly psychoanalytic. I believe that the vast majority of folklore concerns fantasy, and because of that, I am persuaded that techniques of analyzing fantasy are relevant to folklore data. As a realist, I have to confess that my psychoanalytic bias is not shared by many of my folklore colleagues. That is putting it mildly. Let me rephrase the issue. Most folklorists are actively repelled by the application of psychoanalytic theory to folklore. They typically denigrate or ridicule any interpretation with a psychoanalytic cast to it. I bother to mention

the standard academic hostility to psychoanalytic readings of folklore lest some unwary reader assume that the seventh essay is in
any way typical of contemporary folklore research strategy. It is
typical of *my* research, but definitely not of folklorists generally.
After reviewing some of the previous psychoanalytic "treatments"
of the Grimm fairy tale corpus, I try to show by example how psychoanalytic theory can illuminate the content of one particular
tale, namely, "The Maiden Without Hands."

The final essay takes up a ballad enormously popular in the Balkans which tells the tragic tale of a young bride walled up in the
foundation of a castle, bridge, or monastery. She is immured in
order to ensure the successful completion of the constuction project. After surveying the considerable scholarship devoted to the
ballad, I propose a new interpretation of the plot based upon modern feminist-inspired awareness of folklore content.

The variety of genres investigated is intentional on my part. A
folk toy, a weather "proverb," a fairy tale, a ballad—all are examples of the incredibly rich data base offered by folklore. I would
like to think that anyone who reads all the essays in this volume
will come away with a better understanding of what folklore is and
how at least one folklorist goes about studying it. Whether one
agrees with my particular interpretations of the items under discussion is not the issue. What is important is that the exciting field
of folklore become better known and more accessible to a wider
audience. I cannot imagine how anyone discovering folklore and
its study could possibly be interested in anything other than folklore matters.

Acknowledgments

"Defining Identity Through Folklore" first appeared in Anita Jacobson-Widding, ed., *Identity: Personal and Socio-Cultural: A Symposium*, Uppsala Studies in Cultural Anthropology 5 (Uppsala, 1983), 235–61. Reprinted by permission of the Department of Cultural Anthropology, University of Uppsala.

"The Fabrication of Folklore" first appeared as "Nationalistic Inferiority Complexes and the Fabrication of Fakelore: A Reconsideration of Ossian, the *Kinder- und Hausmärchen*, the *Kalevala*, and Paul Bunyan," *Journal of Folklore Research* 22 (1985): 5–18. It is reprinted by permission of the Indiana University Folklore Institute.

"The Anthropologist and the Comparative Method in Folklore" first appeared in *Journal of Folklore Research* 23 (1986): 125–46. It is reprinted by permission of the Indiana University Folklore Institute.

"Pecking Chickens: A Folk Toy as a Source for the Study of Worldview" first appeared as "Pickende Hühner: Thesen zum Weltbild im Spielzeug," *Volkskultur in der Noderne: Probleme und Perspektiven empirischer Kulturforschung*, Utz Jeggle et al.; eds. (Reinbek bei Hamburg: Rowohlt Taschenbuch Verlag, 1986), 323–31. Copyright © 1986 by Tübinger Vereinigung für Volkskunde. Reprinted by permission.

"On Whether Weather 'Proverbs' Are Proverbs" first appeared in *Proverbium* 1 (1984): 39–46, and is reprinted by permission.

"April Fool and April Fish: Towards a Theory of Ritual Pranks" first appeared in *Etnofoor: Anthropologisch Tijdschrift* 1 (1988): 4–14; it is reprinted by permission.

Several of the essays have been slightly revised for publication here.

Defining Identity through Folklore

"Of all relations the most universal is that of identity, being common to every being, whose existence has any duration"
—David Hume, *A Treatise of Human Nature*, 1738.

In the introductory section of James Joyce's *A Portrait of the Artist as a Young Man*, first published in 1916, the protagonist Stephen Dedalus turns to the flyleaf of his geography textbook to read (Joyce 1964: 15–16):

Stephen Dedalus
Class of Elements
Clongowes Wood College
Sallins
County Kildare
Ireland
Europe
The World
The Universe

This traditional, written form of self-identification moves from the individual, as signalled by the personal name, out through a series of identity sets ending with the totality of all things that exist. Such flyleaf inscriptions or book-keepers, as they are sometimes called (to warn others against stealing the book so marked), were evidently appreciated by Joyce, inasmuch as he borrows another example from the same tradition. One of Stephen's friends had inscribed on the opposite page:

Stephen Dedalus is my name,
Ireland is my nation,

1

Clongowes is my dwellingplace,
And heaven my expectation.

A text collected from the north of Ireland around the turn of the century (Bergen 1900:511) demonstrates just how close Joyce was to tradition:

Mary Johnson is my name,
Ireland is my nation,
Clady More's my dwelling-place,
And heaven my expectation.

Flyleaf inscriptions are part of the folklore of literate populations. Although folklorists of the nineteenth century tended to limit the concept of folklore to materials which circulated via oral transmission, twentieth-century folklorists have recognized that there are some kinds of folklore, for example, autograph-book verse, epitaphs, latrinalia (bathroom-wall writings), and xerox folklore (Dundes & Pagter 1975), which are transmitted in written form. Another minor form of written folklore is the envelope sealer commonly used by American adolescents, for example, SWAK (= Sealed with a Kiss). Near the end of Act I of Thornton Wilder's classic play *Our Town*, we find the following piece of dialogue (Wilder 1938:54):

> *Rebecca:* I never told you about that letter Jane Crofut got from her minister when she was sick. The minister of her church in the town she was in before she came here. He wrote Jane a letter and on the envelope the address was like this: It said: Jane Crofut; The Crofut Farm; Grover's Corners; Sutton County; New Hampshire; United States of America.
> *George*: What's funny about that?
> *Rebecca*: But listen, it not finished: the United States of America; Continent of North America; Western Hemisphere; the Earth; the Solar System; the Universe; the Mind of God—that's what it said on the envelope.

This envelope sealer is clearly a variant of the flyleaf inscription utilized by Joyce. What is suggested by these is that one of the ways individuals define their own identity is through folklore.

Scholarly works on identity

The vast scholarship devoted to identity spans most of the disciplines of the social sciences. Topics considered include the anthropological concept of identity (Oliveira 1976:33–51), the philosophical considerations of the relative identity thesis (Noonan 1980), the psychiatric uses of the concept of identity (De Levita 1965), the concept's use in social psychology (Zavalloni 1973, Sarbin & Scheibe 1983) or in sociology (Dashefsky 1972, 1975) or the problems posed by the introduction of the concept of identity in sociology (Taboada-Leonetti 1981), as well as the general nuances and meanings of the words identity, identification, etc. (Schmidt 1976). The popularity of identity as an academic theme is also confirmed by the number of conferences and symposia specifically designed to investigate it, for example, a Wenner-Gren-Sponsored conference on ethnicity in 1970 (De Vos 1975); a symposium on ethnic identity initiated by the Social Science Research Council in 1973 (Royce 1982:24); an interdisciplinary seminar on identity directed by Claude Lévi-Strauss in 1974–1975 (Benoist 1977), an international colloquium at Toulouse in 1979 on "Identités collectives et changements sociaux" (Tap 1980), and a colloquium at Rennes on "L'identité sociale" in 1978 (Kastersztein 1981:95), to mention just a few. In none of the proceedings of these conferences do we find any mention of folklore whatsoever. But, by the same token, we must admit that very few folklorists have paid much attention to the concept of identity (though cf. Bauman 1971, Bausinger 1977 and Honko 1980, 1982, 1988).

The word "identity" derives from the Latin word *idem* meaning "the same," but it has been painfully obvious in all the discussions of the term that its definition depends as much upon differences as upon similarities. One of the earliest statements about identity was made by Heraclitus (*circa* 500 B.C.), when he suggested that a person cannot step into the same river twice. "Same," of course, refers to "identical." Philosophers have been fascinated by rivers ever since. St. Thomas Aquinas wrote as follows:

> The Seine river is not "this particular river" because of "this flowing water," but because of "this source" and "this bed," and hence is

always called the same river although there may be other water flowing down; likewise a people is the same, not because of sameness of soul or of man, but because of the same dwelling place, or because of the same laws or the same manner of living (cited in Noonan 1980:53).

So identity need not mean absolute or perfect identity, as in A = A or as we find in such proverbs as "A bargain is a bargain," "Business is business," "Let bygones be bygones," "Boys will be boys," and "Enough is enough." Locke made much the same point by drawing upon oak-tree and horse analogies rather than a river. In a chapter devoted to "Identity and Diversity" added to the second edition (1694) of *An Essay concerning Human Understanding*, Locke observed, "In the state of living creatures, their identity depends not on a mass of the same particles, but on something else. For in them the variation of great parcels of matter alters not the identity; an oak growing from a plant to a great tree, and then lopped, is still the same oak; and a colt grown up to a horse, sometimes fat, sometimes lean, is all the while the same horse . . ." (1959:442). This metaphor was also employed by David Hume in his chapter "Of Personal Identity" in *A Treatise of Human Nature*, first published in 1738, although he substituted a man for Locke's horse: "An oak that grows from a small plant to a large tree is still the same oak, though there be not one particle of matter or figure of its parts the same. An infant becomes a man, and is sometimes fat, sometimes lean, without any change in his identity" (Hume 1911:243–244). Thus, identity remains constant even if the physical constitutents should change and the same principle can be applied to group identity. "We speak of the same nation as existing through many generations, and of the same corporation as surviving many deaths" (Fullerton 1890:11). Consider the following modern definition of group identity (De Levita 1965:52): "By group identity is meant what a group continues to show as constant features in spite of the fact that the members of the group vary."

Various definitions of identity

The early considerations of identity tended to be more concerned with personal identity than with group identity. Locke, for example, offered a definition of personal identity near the end of the seventeenth century which includes both consciousness and continuity as criteria:

> For, since consciousness always accompanies thinking, and it is that which makes every one to be what he calls self, and thereby distinguishes himself from all other thinking things, in this alone consists personal identity, i.e., the sameness of a rational being: and as far as this consciousness can be extended backwards to any past action or thought, so far reaches the identity of that person; it is the same self now it was then; and it is by the same self with this present one that now reflects on it, that that action was done (1959:449).

One may compare this definition of personal identity with one offered by Erikson, who, among modern thinkers, has been one of the most influential with respect to defining identity (1968:50): "The conscious feeling of having a personal identity is based on two simultaneous observations: the perception of selfsameness and continuity of one's existence in time and space and the perception of the fact that others recognize one's sameness and continuity." Erikson has added the important feature of an individual's awareness that his or her identity is recognized by others. Greenacre (1958:613) makes a similar distinction: "But in general a sense of identity involves some relation to others and has a socially determined component, with a degree of observation both by the person himself and/or through another person." De Levita (1965:150) articulates an extreme form of this position when he says, "In our definition, no one has identity on an uninhabited island, one has it only in so far as one is 'with others.' " (This is reminiscent of the traditional question, "If a tree falls in a forest and no one is there to hear it, is there a sound?")

A mirror metaphor may be helpful here. Greenacre, remarking how important the face is in recognizing the identity of an individual, notes, "As no one ever sees his own face, the nearest he approaches this is the reflection of his face in the water or a mirror" (1958:616). Luckmann extends the mirror metaphor by arguing that each individual acquires personal identity through his reflection from another individual: "Reciprocal mirroring is an elementary condition for the formation of all personal identities" . . . Beginning from childhood, in all societies the self is placed in social relations in which, by virtue of intersubjective mirroring, it is beginning to form a personal identity" (1979:66, 72). This, however, seems to assume that personal identity is a single entity, whereas I would contend that identity, both personal and social, is decidedly multiple in nature. There are many personal identities and many social identities. At some amusement parks, one can find a battery of different mirrors. In one, a person looks tall, in another short, in a third, skinny, a fourth, fat, etc. Which is the real person? I would think that all the images are real in some sense and these diverse mirrors would constitute an apt metaphor for the complexities of multiple personal identities.

It is absolutely essential to understand that it is impossible to speak of sameness without reference to differences, for, if all the members of a given set were identical and the set was equal to the universe, then sameness would be virtually meaningless. This is why teachers of elementary-writing courses invariably give their students the instruction: compare and contrast, that is, find the similarities *and the differences*. There can be no self without other, no identity of group A without a group B. Handelman (1977:189) defines ethnicity in part as the "organization of inclusiveness-exclusiveness," which obviously entails contrast with another group. Recognition by others is just as relevant to definitions of ethnic or other group forms of identity as it is to personal identity. Margaret Mead remarked how people's identity "has depended on defining somebody else's identity. The commonest illustration one can bring up, of course, is the question of how do you define a man if you don't mention a woman. And how do you define a woman if you don't mention a man?" (1958:12).

Spicer, who has written one of the most lucid and insightful essays on identity, goes so far as to suggest that it is an oppositional process which produces or strengthens what he calls "persistent identity systems" (1971:797). Thus, the persecution of minority cultures (for example, Jews, blacks, etc.) by majority cultures has resulted in these oppressed peoples clinging to their identity for dear life. Spicer cites the cases of the Catalans, Basques and Galicians in Spain, but there are hundreds of examples all over the world, for example, the French-speakers in Canada, the Breton-speakers in France, etc. It is this oppositional principle which constitutes one of the common threads in both personal and group identity. As there can be no self or concept of self without other, there can be no sense of group without some other group. Moreover, since minorities experience opposition more than majorities, it is perfectly reasonable that minorities have more of a stake in defining identity (especially their own) than do members of majority cultures.

It is precisely the matter of the relationship of self with others with respect to identity that is critical. Even Erikson, who pioneered the study of what he terms "ego identity," could not avoid this issue. On the one hand, ego identity in its purest form deals only with the self, with the individual. It refers to the sense of sameness or continuity in a given individual throughout the life of that individual (Erikson 1980:22, 94). Sameness and continuity seem to be two of the most common criteria invariably invoked in definitions of identity (De Levita 1965:151). The sense of continuity links the individual with his past. But in his oft-quoted paper "The Problem of Ego Identity," first published in 1956, Erikson admits that the concept of identity cannot be defined without reference to groups of one kind or another. In speaking of Freud's use of the phrase "inner identity," Erikson remarks, "Here, the term 'identity' points to an individual's links with the unique values, fostered by a unique history, of his people" (1980:109). I have already quoted his notion that an individual's identity must be recognized by others, but there is another crucial linkage of self and others with respect to identity. Erikson says further that the term "identity" expresses a mutual relationship "in that it connotes both a persistent sameness within oneself (selfsameness) and a persistent sharing of some kind of essential character with others" (1980:109). But what exactly does "some kind of essential character with others" mean? Here folkloristics has something to contribute to our understanding of identity.

Identity and folklore

There is an important connection between the concept of identity and folklore. Spicer, though he does not use the term "folklore," says, "The essential feature of any identity system is an individual's belief in his personal affiliation with certain symbols, or, more accurately, with what certain symbols stand for. There are collective identity systems as well as individual ones; I am concerned here with collective systems" (1971:795–796). He continues:

> A relationship between human individuals and selected cultural elements—the symbols—is the essential feature of a collective identity system. . . . In addition to land and language symbols, common constituents of identity systems are music, dances, and heroes. What makes a system out of identity symbols is not any logical, in the sense of rational, relationship among them. The meanings that they have fit into a complex that is significant to the people concerned. The meanings amount to a self-definition and an image of themselves as they have performed in the course of their history (Spicer, 1971:796, 798).

Of course, "music, dances and heroes" refers to folklore. What are the vehicles for the communication of a group's symbols? Folklore is clearly one of the most important, perhaps *the* most important, sources for the articulation and perpetuation of a group's symbols. Bauman stated this premise well when he observed "Folklore is a function of shared identity" (1971:32).

Max Weber in his discussion of ethnic groups (1968:385–398) makes repeated reference to "customs." For instance, he says, "We shall call 'ethnic groups' those human groups that entertain a subjective belief in their common descent because of similarities of physical type or of customs or both . . ." (1968:389). He notes also, "Pronounced differences of custom, which play a role equal to that of inherited physical type in the creation of feelings of common ethnicity and notions of kinship, are usually caused, in addition to linguistic and religious differences, by the diverse economic and political conditions of various social groups" (1968:392). Whether or not we accept the idea that customs are truly caused by economic and political factors, it is of considerable interest that Max Weber fastens upon customs as being crucial with respect to defining ethnicity. For what are customs if not a standard genre of folklore?

Let us consider George DeVos's succinct definition of an ethnic group: "An ethnic group is a self-perceived group of people who hold in common a set of traditions not shared by the others with whom they are in contact" (1975:9). What is meant by traditions? Surely they include the folklore of that group. DeVos says this, although he too does not mention the word "folklore." "In brief, the ethnic identity of a group of people consists of their subjective symbolic or emblematic use of any aspect of culture, in order to differentiate themselves from other groups. . . . Ethnic features such as language or clothing or food can be considered emblems, for they show others who one is and to what group one belongs" (1975:116). If one substituted folk speech, costume and food habits for language, clothing and food, it would perhaps be more obvious that it is folklore which is responsible in large measure for creating ethnic identity.

Spicer's "music, dances, and heroes," Weber's "customs," and DeVos's "traditions" all fall under the rubric of folklore. Folklore includes myths, folktales, legends, proverbs, riddles, folk beliefs, costume, folk medicine, traditional foods, folk speech, charms, curses, games, folk music, folk dances, etc. The idea that folklore can express a group's identity is not a new one. Indeed, it was Herder who claimed centuries ago that the soul of a people was expressed in that people's folk-songs (Ergang 1931:198; Clark 1969:249). One of Erikson's Sioux informants gave an admirably concise definition of identity which shows how an individual is linked to his group through tradition: "The way you see me now is the way I really am, and it is the way of my forefathers" (Erikson 1963:129).

Folklore research

There are dozens of modern illustrations of Herder's view. Consider the following appreciation of the Latvian folk-songs called *dainas*: "It should be noted that to the Latvian the *dainas* are more than a literary tradition. They are the very embodiment of his cultural heritage, left by forefathers whom history had denied other, more tangible forms of expression. These songs thus form the very core of the Latvian identity and singing becomes one of the identifying qualities of a Latvian" (Vikis-Freibergs 1975:19). Recall that continuity is one of the key criteria in defining identity. In this light, we can remark that "the *dainas* have become a main avenue to finding a sense of continuity with those who have gone before, a continuity which can contribute a deeper meaning to one's present identity" (Vikis-Freibergs 1975:20). It would be easy to multiply examples. In Yugoslavia, Slovenian children's-book writers have turned to folklore as inspirational source material. "The quest of cultural identity is at the core of their determination to emphasize the mother tongue and the native folk tradition of Slovenia" (Kamenetsky 1974:1441). Similarly, we find that, among the peoples of Senegal, it has been suggested that folklore may be the principal insurer of cultural identity (N'Diaye 1980:17). The Latvian and Slovenian examples also serve to remind us that it is precisely those nations, or groups within nations, that have been most anxious about their own identity that have been the most active in carrying out folklore research. It is surely no accident that some of the most intensive folklore-collecting in the world has taken place in Ireland and Finland (cf. Honko 1980). The rise of folkloristics as a discipline is intimately associated with the growth of nationalism (and romanticism) in the nineteenth century.

I believe the concept of "folk" itself may be helpful in the study of identity. The bulk of identity scholarship has tended to focus either on the self or on the group, especially the ethnic group. There can be no question that self-identity or personal identity is a legitimate subject for any serious theoretical treatment of identity, but, by the same token, it is a great over-simplification to limit discussions of identity to "self." Similarly, important as ethnic identity may be, it is only one type of identity, that is, one type of group identity. The confusion surrounding the concept of ethnic group can be illustrated by mentioning three so-called ethnic groups in the United States: Chicanos, Jews, and blacks. Just with these three groups, we have criteria of national origin, religious affiliation, and race. In what sense, if any, is it appropriate to speak of these three groups as *ethnic* groups? There is also confusion between ethnic and national groups. Italians are a national group and Italian-Americans are an ethnic group, but surely there is some overlap between these two groups. Many ethnic groups are historically related to national groups. In other words, so-called minority groups in one cultural setting may have been majority groups in the original homeland.

Ethnic groups

I am not the first to complain about the fuzziness of the conceptualization of ethnicity. Isaacs (1975:30) jokingly refers to "the snowman of 'ethnicity,' whose footprints have been around us for so long but which has been so curiously difficult for academic hunters to track down." Let me attempt to show how the concept of folk avoids some of the pitfalls inevitable in the use of "ethnic group." Folk is not a synonym for peasant (as it was in the nineteenth century), nor is it limited to one stratum of society, for example, the *vulgus in populo*, or the lower class. Nor is it the illiterate in a literate society (cf. Hultkrantz 1960:126–129). The term "folk" can refer to *any group of people whatsoever* who share at least one common factor. It does not matter what the linking factor is—it could be a common occupation, language or religion—what is important is that a group formed for whatever reason will have some traditions which it calls its own. In theory, a group must consist of at least two persons, but generally most groups consist of many individuals. A member of the group may not know all other members, but he will probably know the common core of traditions belonging to the group, traditions which help the group to have a sense of group identity. If the group were composed of lumberjacks or railroadmen, then the folklore would be lumberjack or railroadmen folklore. If the group were composed of Jews or blacks, then the folklorist could seek Jewish or black folklore. Probably the smallest group would be an individual family, whose traditions often include sayings and such items as a family whistle (to call or locate a family member lost in a crowd). We can see that a folk is a much more flexible concept than ethnic group. A folk can be as small as a family and as large as a nation. An ethnic group would simply be one type of folk, but by no means the only type. (See "Who are the Folk?" in Dundes 1980:1–19.)

The utilization of "folk" in place of "ethnic group" would considerably broaden the base of theoretical discussions of identity, beyond the unfortunately overly restrictive limits of ethnic group. For one thing, the modern definition of folk allows one to think of individuals belonging simultaneously to many different and distinct folk groups. He or she is at once a member of a family, ethnic group, religious group, occupational group, nation, etc., and is familiar with the folklore of each of these groups. Moreover, the individual must often learn to code-switch, as he or she moves from one group to another. One would not normally use the folk-speech lexicon of one's military-reserve unit while carrying on a conversation with the members of one's church group.

Zavalloni (1973:66, 82) has given a valuable list of social categories which she terms "identity groups": "A minimal account will include one's national and ethnic membership, religion, sex, occupation, social class, age, family status and political-party affiliation." However, there are many folk groups which are not included in that comprehensive list. For example, most of the groups enumerated in the flyleaf and envelope address cited at the beginning of this essay would be left out. Most individuals, I suspect, do define part of their identity with respect to "place." But it is much more complicated than simply being from a particular village or town or city or from a particular state or province. And this brings us to two of the most serious deficiencies in previous discussions of identity. Most notions of identity tend to be static and absolute instead of being flexible and relative. We can see this most easily by recalling one of the principal testing devices designed to measure or gauge identity: the "Who am I?" test. In such a test, individuals are asked to write down twenty or so labels which they think would properly answer the question. Erikson (1968:314) has protested the use of the test, saying "I must register a certain impatience with the faddish equation, never suggested by me, of the term identity with the question 'Who am I?' . . . The pertinent question, if it can be put into the first person at all, would be 'What do I want to make of myself, and what do I have to work with?'" I think Erikson may be a bit too hard on the test (for more on the "Who am I?" approach to identity, see Kuhn & McPartland 1954, Zavalloni 1973:77–797, Hooper 1976, and Taboada-Leonetti 1981:141–143), but it should be obvious that answers to such a question would depend in part upon who was asking the question and where and when the question was being asked. The "Who am I?" test should be given to the same individual at different times and places in his or her life. An individual's sense of identity changes throughout the life cycle and these changes might be registered by re-testing. It would also be interesting to note the rank ordering of the responses, for example, does one put nationality before religious affiliation, or family role before occupational group? And does this rank ordering of identities change through time when the test is re-administered to the same individuals?

Context and identity

The importance of context to identity (or at least the out-group labelling of such) is encapsulated in the following racist, riddling question: "When does a black become a nigger?" Answer: "When he leaves the room." The relativity of identity would be evident if I were to attempt to answer the question "Who am I?" with respect to where I was from. If I were in Europe, I might say I am an American or I am from the States. In New York, I might say I was a Californian. In Los Angeles, I might say I was from the Bay area (that is, from northern California, as opposed to southern California, where Los Angeles is located). In San Francisco, I might say I was from Berkeley. In Berkeley, I might say I was from the north side (of the campus of the University of California). In my own neighborhood in Berkeley, I might say that I lived at the top of Cedar (Street) on La Vereda. I feel that part of my identity is defined as a resident of La Vereda on the north side of Berkeley in the Bay area, in California, in the United States. My impression is that most of the published research reports on identity somehow tend to suggest that there is an absolute, unchanging feature of identity. I submit that many features of identity are relative, relative to particular social or interactional settings. The sense of identity tied to "place" in any case is not easily subsumed under the concept of ethnic group, yet place can be, and often is, an extremely meaningful component of individual identity.

Another difficulty with much of the conceptualization of identity stems from the failure to distinguish between permanent and temporary identities. Some forms of identity (but not all) are permanent and unchanging. Isajiw (1974:120) refers to this factor as "involuntary," but a word implying volition or its lack is not really the *mot juste* in my opinion. Sex and race, for example, one cannot really change. Isajiw includes "social class" as an instance of an involuntary group, but I would maintain that social class can be changed by an individual in his lifetime. (In fact, I think that it is interesting that anyone can claim that social class is the same order of involuntary identity factor as race!) Isajiw offers a definition of ethnicity as "an involuntary group of people who share the same culture or to descendants of such people who identify themselves and/or are identified by others as belonging to the same involuntary group" (1974:122). He includes religious groups as involuntary, but, as many religions allow for conversion, I should think that such groups would be better categorized as voluntary associations. De Levita, borrowing from the anthropologist Linton's distinction between ascribed and achieved status, speaks of "ascribed identials (age, sex, origin, nationality, social class, in short, any membership a group which one cannot choose for oneself)" (1965:169) and "achieved or adopted identity" (1965:-183–184). He too designates social class as ascribed, which perhaps suggests that Europeans, as opposed to Americans, have a different view of social mobility with respect to class structure. Barth (1969:28) distinguishes between ascription (involving criteria or origin and commitment) and performance (referring to acting roles required to realize identity).

Let me cite one example of a type of identity omitted in conventional definitions which shows the irrelevance of the voluntary/involuntary distinction. The identity in question is that of belonging to one of the districts or wards of the city of Siena in Tuscany. Inhabitants of Siena feel incredibly strong attachments to their district, which is called a *contrada*. Each of the seventeen *contrade* has its own name, for example, *Oca* (goose), *Giraffa* (giraffe), *Civetta* (owl), etc. (colors, government, territorial boundaries, songs, etc.). The *contrada* is a cross between an extended family (with a virtual totemic symbol) and a minipolitical entity. A Sienese considers himself first and foremost a *contradaiolo*, a member of his or her *contrada*. Outside the city, speaking to a hated rival Florentine, he may consider himself Sienese, but, within Siena, he definitely feels himself one of the *Brucaioli* (caterpillars), *Panterini* (panthers), *Tartuchini* (turtles), etc. A member of the Tower *contrada* would never dream of wearing clothes of the colors (red and green) of the arch-rival, Goose *contrada*, just as Goose *contrada* members would never wear the burgundy colors of the Tower *contrada*. The *contrada* identity is displayed in costume and in competition in the celebrated festival of the *palio*, a horse-race held twice each summer in honor of the Virgin Mary. It is the *contrada* which competes in the race and the members of the winning *contrada* may suck pacifiers after the race to signify their joy (and rebirth). It would not be an exaggeration to say that the primary social group with which most individual Sienese identify is the *contrada*. In theory, one is born into the *contrada*, but one can also be baptized into the *contrada* and even foreigners (from other countries) can become *contrada* members (for more details about the *contrada*, see Dundes & Falassi 1975:12–47).

So a Sienese might on one occasion be an Italian (in speaking to a Frenchman), a Tuscan (in speaking to a Neapolitan), a Sienese (in speaking to a Florentine) or a Goose (in speaking to a Giraffe). National and ethnic categories would not accommodate all of these distinctions, but each of them would certainly constitute a separate folk group. One could speak of Italian folklore, Tuscan folklore, Sienese folklore, and even Goose folklore. Membership of different folk groups also allows for what has been called "identity-switching" (Lyman & Douglass 1973:357–358). Just as there are bilinguals, there are also biculturals, individuals who belong to two or more folk groups (for example, his parents may be from different groups). A striking example of identity options is the following:

> The Basque people (whose Old World homeland encompasses a portion of both Spain and France) in America provides several examples of this phenomenon. When interacting with fellow ethnics from Spain, a Spanish-born Basque is likely to invoke his regional subethnic identity—e.g., to remind his audience that he is a *Vizcayan*; with fellow ethnics from France his *national* ethnic identity—e.g., a Spanish Basque; with non-Basques, his general ethnic identity—e.g., a *Basque*; with Old World Basques on a return trip to the Pyrenees region, his adopted civic and social identity—e.g., and *Amerikanue* (Lyman & Douglass, 1973:355).

In the same way, one could speak of different folk groups: Spanish-Basque, French-Basque, Basque, and Basque-Americans all have different (though related) folklore repertoires.

Folklore and sexual identity

Regardless of whether or not one can see the advantages of employing the modern definition of folk in lieu of the more limited concept of ethnic group with respect to studying the onion-skin layering of the multiple identities of each individual, there should be no hesitation in having recourse to the materials of folklore to better understand the nature of identity. Let me illustrate with several examples just how folklore defines identity.

Sexual identity is one of the first types of identity to be socially recognized. In fact, elaborate folk-divination techniques are employed to ascertain the sex of an unborn baby. So, even before birth, there may be some discussion of the forthcoming infant in terms of sex, for example, what name to give him or her (cf. McCartney [1922] for the antiquity of sex-divination techniques). Upon birth, a baby in the United States is typically put into pink or blue baby clothes, depending upon its sex. Pink, a pale, weak, passive color, is for girls; blue, a strong, primary color, is for boys. Sexual identity is color-coded right from the start. And sexual identity is maintained through folklore. Girls play jacks and jump rope; boys usually do not play these traditional games. Boys play mumbletypeg (involving the throwing of a jackknife from various parts of the body so that the blade sticks straight in the earth); girls ordinarily do not.

During adolescence, a form of folklore known as a "catch" may be employed to ensure the absolute separation of male and female sexual identity. In this connection, it is noteworthy that Robert Bak in commenting on Greenacre's paper on identity contended that "the wish to repudiate or change one's sex is one of the major identity problems of puberty" (Rubenfine 1958:135). A person may be asked how he or she looks at his or her fingernails. Supposedly, boys make a fist (palm up) to observe their nails, while girls hold out their hand (palm down) inclined at an upward angle for the same purpose. Boys look at their heels by turning their feet outward and looking down in front of them; girls do this by pointing their toes down and looking back over their shoulders to view their heels. Boys extinguish a match by shaking it several times, while girls purse their lips and blow it out. Boys throw a ball overhand, while girls throw underhand. In the United States, how one crosses one's legs is critical. Women cross one leg over the other, so that the two knees are touching; men put one leg over the other, so that the ankle of the raised, akimbo leg rests behind the kneecap of the stationary leg. In similar fashion, women usually carry books on their chests, cradled by arms crossed and clasped at the waist, while men carry books on their sides held by hands or under the arm. There are many more of these gestural tests of sexual identity which are commonly used by high-school students to catch or embarrass their peers of both sexes, but these should suffice to demonstrate the connection between folklore and identity, in this case, sexual identity. It should be pointed out that these gestural catches can be traced back in time. For instance, a boy in a sitting position will catch an object thrown into his lap by pulling his two legs together, whereas a girl will spread her legs (so that her skirt will better form a receptacle to receive the object). Mark Twain borrowed this device in *The Adventures of Huckleberry Finn* as a way of revealing Huck's disguise as a girl. Huck pulls his legs together and is recognized as a boy by Mrs Loftus, who then offers this explanation to Huck:

> You do a girl tolerable poor, but you might fool men, maybe. Bless you, child, when you set out to thread a needle, don't hold the thread still and fetch the needle up to it; hold the needle still and poke the thread at it; that's the way a woman most always does, but a man always does t'other way. . . . And, mind you, when a girl tries to catch anything in her lap she throws her knees apart; she don't clap them together the way you did when you catched the lump of lead. Why, I spotted you for a boy when you was threading the needle; and I contrived the other things just to make certain (Twain 1948:61).

The date of *Huckleberry Finn's* publication, 1884, gives us a useful *terminus ante quem* for this neglected, minor genre of folklore.

It is sometimes wrongly assumed by students of identity that identity loss necessarily constitutes a period of crisis commonly called an identity crisis. But identity *per se* is neither positive nor negative. Some members of some groups are unhappy with their identity and consciously want to change that identity. There are Americans who want to be Europeans, as well as Europeans who want to be Americans. There are Jews who want to be gentiles and occasionally gentiles who want to be Jews. There are boys who want to be girls and girls who want to be boys. There are children who want to be adults and, yes, adults who want to be children. Folklore, as fantasy, often provides a socially sanctioned outlet for the expression of such wishful thinking.

Adopting a different identity may be voluntarily engaged in, but sometimes identity changes are imposed on individuals. For example, in some cultures, parents fearful of malevolent powers or disease may try to disguise the sexual identity of their children. "A new-born boy may be proclaimed to be a girl for such prophylactic purposes in India . . . while among the Sakai-Jakun of Pahang, a boy may have his ears bored for ear-studs in order to make him appear to be a girl, when a mother has been unlucky in losing all her boy infants previously" (Balfour 1924:21). There are also instances in urban cultures when identity changes or "loss" can be desirable. It is certainly positive in the story of the student at a final examination who continues to write after the professor has collected the examination booklets from all the other students. Fifteen or twenty minutes after the examination is over, the student rushes up to the professor to turn in his booklet. "I'm sorry," says the professor, "but it is too late to turn in the examination now. I will not accept it." "Do you know who I am?" asks the student (with an intonation hinting that he may be someone important with influential friends in high places). "No, I do not," replies the professor. "Good," says the student and slips his booklet right into the middle of the pile of examinations. The joke suggests that sometimes anonymity has its advantages.

Games, another major genre of folklore, offer opportunities for the assumption of another identity. For example, in a popular guessing game played at parties, the host will place on the back of each guest who arrives some picture or a name of a celebrity. The object of the game is for each individual to guess his new identity. (He does this by asking others, who can see the picture on his back, questions about this assumed identity). In another party game, when those present know one another fairly well, a person designated as "it" is sent out of the room. In his absence, the others sitting in a circle agree to assume the identity of the person sitting immediately to their left (or right). When "it" returns to the room, he must pose personal questions to each member of the circle and try to figure out what has happened. Each individual questioned answers the question as though he or she were the person to his or her immediate left.

Many forms of folklore play on identity confusion. Remember that the theme of false or mistaken identity, often accomplished through the presence of twins, is a common theme in literature, for example, plays. The riddle genre offers numerous instances. A man points to a photograph of a man and says, "Brothers and sisters have I none, yet this man's father is my father's son." Who is the person in the picture? (It is a picture of the son of the speaker.) A more striking instance is the incest riddle often found in the oral versions of the Oedipus tale. Consider the following quatrain from an Albanian folk-tale:

Hush thee, hush thee, son!
Son of my son!
Son of my daughter-in-law!
Born to thy father-in-law!

The quatrain is sung by a woman to her child, as they both die by the hand of her elder son, whom she has unwittingly married.

The meaning of the first two lines requires no gloss, and that of the third little; as her elder son's wife, the woman is daughter-in-law to his mother, that is, to herself. Consequently, the baby is her daughter-in-law's child. The fourth line is extremely involved. As the mother of her married son, the woman is mother-in-law to his wife, again herself. As her husband, her elder son is father-in-law where she is mother-in-law, and since she is her own mother-in-law, he is her father-in-law. Consequently, the baby is the child of a man who is son, husband, and father-in-law to one and the same woman, and she again is her own daughter-in-law and her own mother-in-law (Hasluck, 1949:340).

Here indeed is a remarkable example of identity being defined through folklore, in this case, a riddle in a folk-tale.

A text from the early 1970s presents a slightly less complex identity puzzle. A man and his son are in a serious automobile accident. The man is killed, but the boy is rushed to the emergency room of the nearest hospital. When he is brought into the operating room, the surgeon says, "I cannot operate on this boy because he is my son." How can this be? Answer: the surgeon is a woman, the boy's mother. This text is a bit more socially relevant to feminism than such older examples as: "A blind beggar had a brother who died, but the man who died had no brother. What was the relationship of the two?" The key to this apparent paradox lies in the beggar being female and hence the sister of the man who died. Such puzzles could not exist without the difficulty of thinking of generic surgeons and beggars as anything but male figures.

Temporary changes of identity

Perhaps the most striking examples of folklore's providing an outlet for temporary identity change are furnished by festival or holiday customs. For instance, American Halloween is a time when children dress up in outlandish costumes and wear masks. Often, boys will dress up as girls and girls will dress up as boys. This time of ritual reversals permits a disguise of identity, including sex change through dress. Part of the fun of this holiday is precisely the temporary alteration of one's day-to-day identity. Identity loss in this case is not unpleasurable.

To be sure, some losses of identity can be painful. Birth might be said to be the first, traumatic, identity loss. Without better fetal research, it is difficult to say just when selfhood begins, but, in one sense, it certainly begins at birth, when the neonate is rudely separated from its mother and its umbilical cord is cut. Before that, mother and child share a common identity. It may well be that the newly born infant has no consciousness of itself (De Levita 1965:36; Greenacre 1958:615), and in fact folkloristic custom at-

tempts in one way to simulate the womb-like existence lost by placing infants in cradles, some of which rock in a fashion not unlike
the motion of being carried inside the mother's body. But the
point is that life begins with the loss of one identity and the acqui-
sition of another. Life continues in much the same way, as different identities are variously acquired and some shed.

An individual may and will maintain different identities at the
same time. A woman may be a granddaughter, daughter, sister,
cousin, aunt, niece, mother and grandmother—all at once. We
know that any one individual lies at the intersection of a large
number of distinct kinship relations and that the individual identifies with one or all of these relations. One has identity as a sister,
as a daughter, as a mother, etc. One may be a female and a daughter at birth, but some of the other identities can only be assumed
through the process of living. (I am speaking here of identities,
not roles. One can have the identity of a sister regardless of what
role one plays with that identity.)

Identity in folk-tales

The importance of identity can be observed in folk-tales. In Vladimir Propp's remarkable analysis of the structure of Russian fairy-
tales, in which he distinguished thirty-one functions (units of plot
action), he included function XVII, the hero is branded, and function XXVII, the hero is recognized. Typically, the hero or heroine
is recognized by the mark or wound that he or she received earlier.
In the majority of tales, the recognition scene allows the protagonist to prove his or her proper identity, which leads inevitably to
the final function XXXI, the hero is married and ascends the
throne. One large segment of the "H. Tests" section of the six-
volume *Motif-Index of Folk-Literature* consists of identity tests
(recognition). The recognition may be accomplished by scar
(H51), birthmark (H51.1), branding (H55), by tokens (H80), by
a ring (H94), by a broken weapon (H101) or by garment (H111).
One common suitor task is to choose the princess from others
identically clad (H324). This is normally accomplished by means
of a pre-arranged signal (H161). In folk-tales, we are reminded
that identity itself is neither good nor bad. In Oedipus (Aarne-

Thompson tale-type 931), the hero does indeed establish his identity, and in most oral versions through his having been marked or scarred as a child, but surely the process of learning his true identity is a painful and tragic one. On the other hand, in Cinderella (Aarne-Thompson tale-type 510A), the heroine demonstrates her true identity in a happier fashion, for example, when the famous glass slipper fits her foot and her foot alone.

We can see in fairy-tale structure that self-identity is tied to group recognition of identity. Cinderella, the household drudge who sits, dirty and disfigured, by the hearth, is the same person as the dazzlingly beautiful belle of the ball, but it is only when the outside world realizes this fact that the tale's dénouement, her happy marriage, can be achieved. In like fashion, Oedipus is both the infant who at birth was destined to kill his father and marry his mother and the young man who, unknowingly raised by foster-parents, does fulfill his predicted fate. But it is both his *and* the outside world's recognition of his identity that gives the plot its dramatic impact.

The images of males and females in fairy-tales and other forms of folklore may be idealized and may involve stereotypes, for example, the passive princess who gets into difficulties and has to wait for an active prince to rescue her. It could well be argued that one of the most important links between folklore and identity has to do with stereotypes. The distinctive, character trait of any identity set—no matter whether the set is based on sex, nationality, ethnicity, religious affiliation, occupation, etc.—is very probably the subject (or object) of stereotyping. There is self-concept, but also self-stereotype; national character and also national stereotype; ethnic character and ethnic stereotype. Self-stereotype and ethnic/national stereotypes are interrelated, just as personal identity and group identity are.

National stereotypes

One might conceivably argue whether or not there is such a thing as national character (for references to the enormous, national-character scholarship, see Dundes 1981), but there can be absolutely no question that there are such things as national stereotypes (Dundes 1975). Ample evidence from folklore can easily document the existence of stereotypes. It could even be seriously maintained that folklore provides one of the principal sources for the articulation and communication of stereotypes. An individual may gain his first impression of a national or ethnic or religious or racial group by hearing traditional jokes or expressions referring to the alleged personality characteristics of that group. Whether or not there is a so-called "kernel of truth" in stereotypes is debatable, but there is some reason for thinking that there may be some overlap (though not total congruence) between national character and national stereotype. There is also the issue of possible overlap between self-stereotype and national stereotype. For example, the Germans see themselves as militaristic and members of other European nations frequently depict the Germans in such terms. Consider the following, standard, international, multi-group slur (Dundes 1975:32):

> There is an international congress on the elephant and scholars from different countries present their learned communications:
> The Englishman gives his paper on "Elephant-Hunting in India."
> The Russian presents "The Elephant and the Five-Year Plan."
> The Italian offers "The Elephant and the Renaissance."
> The Frenchman delivers "Les amours des éléphants" (or, in some versions, "L'éléphant dans la cuisine").
> The German gives "The Elephant and the Renazification of Germany" (or, in other versions, "The Military Use of the Elephant" or "A Short Introduction to the Life of Four-footed Elephants"—in 24 volumes but he dies after preparing the seventeenth volume for press).
> And finally the American rises to give his paper on "How to Build a Bigger and Better Elephant."

Most European countries boast versions of this joke, though with different nationalities and stereotypes represented. In fact, it is interesting to see which nationalities are selected by which countries to be represented in the joke text, as well as which stereotypic traits are attributed to them. Compare a Norwegian version of the elephant-conference joke (Dundes 1975:34):

> The German: 150 Ways to Use the Elephant for War
> The Frenchman: The Sex Life of the Elephant
> The American: The Biggest Elephant I Ever Saw

The Swede: The Political and Social Organization of the Elephant
The Dane: 150 Ways to Cook an Elephant
And, finally, the Norwegian gives his paper entitled: "Norway and We Norwegians".

One reason for the possible overlap between stereotype and character is the self-fulfilling prophecy factor. For example, in the United States, fat people are not necessarily innately jolly, but, upon learning that fat people are assumed to be jolly, a corpulent individual might feel obliged to act out the stereotype and, by so doing, make behavior conform to the stereotype. Here, folklore can be an influential, though not always desirable, factor in shaping identity.

It is also true that individuals may actively struggle against their stereotype. One Afro-American informant very much aware of the notion of CP time (Colored Person's time), meaning some unspecified time after an agreed-upon, fixed time, in other words, that Afro-Americans tend to be late in keeping appointments, claimed that she made a virtual fetish out of being early or on time for engagements, just because she did not want to risk conforming to the stereotype.

Negative identity features

Sometimes it is the internalization of stereotypes by a minority group which can cause problems in identity. Erikson observed that every person's "psycho-social identity" contains both positive and negative elements (1968:303). These negative elements, caused or, at any rate, reinforced by stereotypes held by members of other groups, can lead to self-hate, as it is termed. Thus, Jews may come to hate their Jewishness and blacks may come to hate their blackness, or so the theory goes (see, for example, Lewin 1941; Kardiner & Ovesey 1962, Gilman 1986:1–21). Kardiner & Ovesey (297, n. 3) go so far as to say that "self-hatred in varying degrees is a constant feature in all minority groups." What happens supposedly is that the minority group accepts the majority group's stereotype. Doubt has been expressed about the validity of the self-hate construct. For example, Zavalloni (1973:69) points out the difficulties and also observes that (85), "A person can have negative views of his own group, but this does not necessarily imply self-hatred." Still, negative views of one's own group is a serious enough matter, regardless of whether one wishes to call such views self-hate. There does seem to be evidence, for example, that colonized people have accepted the idea that they do have the traits attributed to them by their colonizers, for example, that they are lazy, docile, incompetent or ugly, or that women see themselves as maternal, intuitive, incapable of abstract reasoning, etc. (Taboada-Leonetti 1981:153; cf. N'Diaye (1980:4) and Eidheim's discussion (1969) of Lappish identity in Norway in terms of social stigma). If self-hate is truly a part of personal identity, then the interrelationship between personal identity and group identity is once again clear-cut. Self-hate could not arise without input from others.

In terms of folklore, it is pertinent that sometimes negative identity features are turned to advantage. A remarkable legend collected in 1939 in Harlem under the auspices of the Federal Writers' Project by Ralph Ellison from Leo Gurley demonstrates this. In the legend (Levine 1977:405–406), a trickster named Sweet-the-monkey, living in Florence, South Carolina ("one of these hard towns on colored folks"), had an incredible skill ("Sweet could make hisself invisible"). He used his invisibility to rob white folks and to escape from them when he was caught. It is not possible to convey the vitality of the legend in a paraphrase. What is interesting in the present context is that Ellison was to go on to write his memorable novel *Invisible Man*, published in 1952 about a young black man's search for identity. There can be little doubt that the central metaphor of invisibility was inspired by the legend that Ellison had collected. In the south, blacks were treated by whites as though they were invisible. Whites held conversations with one another in the presence of blacks (servants), but they acted as if the blacks were invisible, that is, as though they were not persons, as though they had no identity. In the legend, the invisible nature of blacks *vis-à-vis* whites becomes a black trickster's means of robbing the whites "blind."

A minority group cannot always find support for its identity in the majority community. White folklore, symbolized by the fairy tale of Snow *White*, reflects white society and white esthetics and values, not black. One thinks of the young black girl who addresses a question to the magic mirror on the wall: "Mirror, mirror on the wall, who's the fairest one of all?" And the mirror answers: "Snow White, you black bitch, and don't you forget it" (Dundes 1973:638). Surely, part of the point of this black joke is that blacks should not expect to receive ego support from white folklore with its magical mirrors which continue to reflect the same old prejudice—black is evil (as in blackmail, black list, black sheep, etc.), in contrast to white which is good—even a lie is acceptable if it is white! Victimized by the color semiotic, blacks sought to create new folklore extolling black: "Black is beautiful!" But the battle is an uphill one. A solidly positive proverb like "The blacker the berry, the sweeter the juice" also exists in variant forms with such pessimistic addenda as "But if you're too damn black, it ain't no use," which is reminiscent of the classic "self-hate" rhyme in Afro-American tradition: "If you're white, you're all right; if you're brown, stick around; but if you're black, get back" (Dundes 1973:12). These are examples of folklore which shape identity, although the identity is negative.

Sometimes black folklore is even usurped by whites—this has been the case from Stephen Foster's music to the Beatles. Afro-American music when performed by whites has lined the pockets of the white performers. It is sad to see the misappropriation of a group's folklore, especially when the group's own folklore is used to perpetuate a negative stereotype of that group. Consider the case of John Henry, one of the few black, folklore heroes known to the white community. In the popular song and legend, John Henry's master or employer bets that John Henry can drive more steel or drill through a tunnel faster than a new, steel driving machine or steam-drill. In most versions, John Henry wins but dies in the effort, achieving at best a Pyrrhic victory. Erikson in "Reflections on the American Identity" (1963:285–325), one of the relatively few discussions of identity which makes any mention of folklore, repeats the standard white interpretation of the story as man's triumph over the machine, a true testament to the nobility of the human spirit (299). But, upon closer inspection, I believe that this widely accepted white reading of John Henry's story merely confirms the white's wishful stereotypic thinking about blacks, especially black males. Here we have a powerful black man who dies doing the white man's work. Although he is incredibly strong, he is not militant, not aggressive. In terms of the white stereotype of the super-phallic, black male, John Henry dies with "his hammer in his hand," hardly a threat to white womanhood. In many Afro-American versions of the folksong, the final stanza tells that:

> This old hammer
> Killed John Henry
> Can't kill me,
> Can't kill me.

This may suggest that the modern black man will not die doing the white man's dirty work and that also perhaps his phallic power cannot be checked (cf. Dundes 1973:561–577).

The folklore of identity

The folklore of identity includes both indications of desire to change one's identity and of the realization that it may be impossible to make such changes. In the United States, one way in which new immigrants have nominally sought to change their identity is through a name change, for example, an Anglicization of their original surname. This tendency is the topic of the following Jewish joke:

> There was this Jew by the name of Mikifsky, who wanted to change his name to Murphy. So he went to a judge and had it changed. A year later though, the man went back to the same judge and asked to have his name changed again from Murphy to O'Brien. The judge said, "Why? Murphy is a good Irish name." And the man replied, "I want to have something to say when people ask me what my name was before I changed it."

To be sure, anti-Semitism in Europe and elsewhere did encourage Jews to try to conceal their identity, but the point here is that no one is really fooled by such a change. Until the formation of Israel, Jews have always been a minority people trying to survive. Part of adapting to conform to the country where they resided included name changes. It is of interest that the judge does not question the initial name-change request—Mikifsky is simply not a prestigious name, but there is nothing wrong with a good Irish name like Murphy! In any case, the fact that people insisted upon asking what the protagonist's name was before he changed it suggests that he has been unsuccessful in trying to conceal other facets of his Jewish identity. In this sense, the joke is typical. The Jew tries to change his identity, but he is unable to do so. (For a Mexican-name-change joke, see Limón 1977:37–38.)

Another representative illustration of the same identity issue plays upon the theme that a Jew cannot convert to Christianity, no matter how hard he may try:

> Do you know the one about the little, old, devout, Orthodox Jew who decides in the latter part of his life to turn to Catholicism? Well, the Catholic Church is so delighted, because this is wonderful propaganda for the universal appeal of the Church, and they invite him to speak at the next congregation. So the little Jew gets up and says, "Fellow goyim . . ." (Dundes 1971:196).

Goyim is the plural form of *goy*, the Yiddish word for gentiles, non-Jews. The joke, enjoyed by Jews, confirms the fact that some Jews seek to become Christians (cf. the "Jews for Jesus" movement in the United States), but at the same time, it reassures the in-group that Jewishness cannot be renounced. The term *goyim* often has a slightly pejorative connotation (Rosten 1970:142), a fact of which Margaret Mead may have been unaware. In an address entitled "Israel and Problems of Identity" which she gave at the Theodor Herzl Institute in New York City in October 1957, she referred to herself as follows: "You realize, of course, I am speaking as a *goy*, who has a *goishe kopf*" (Mead 1958:2). One has the feeling that Mead thinks the term is simply one denoting out-group.

On occasion, the Jews' defense against the attempts of Christians to convert them involves a pointed reminder of the Jewish origin of Christianity or of Jesus in particular. In a modern text of the early 1980s: "How do we know that Jesus was Jewish? Answer: Because he lived at home (unmarried) until he was 30, he went into his father's business, and his mother thought he was God."

Folklore, through the psychological mechanism of projective inversion (Dundes 1980:51–55), also allows a group's fear that its young may be converted to resemble the out-group to be transformed into the idea that it will be the majority group which loses its identity by resembling the minority group, at least with respect to language or dialect:

> A Jewish family sent their son to a fashionable boarding-school to learn good English.
>
> "Please, you being sure titch him right," the father told the headmaster.
>
> "You need not have the slightest concern whatsoever," replied the headmaster. [In some versions, the headmaster says, "Fear not. When you return at the end of the semester, you will not be able to distinguish your son's pronunciation from my own."]
>
> At the end of the school year, the father called on the headmaster. "Und how is my boy doink?"
>
> "Dun't esk!" said the headmaster (Dorson 1960:166–168).

It may not just be the majority group which is converted, so to speak, but even other minority groups may be influenced by the presumed strength of the joke-teller's group's identity. The following Jewish joke contains a striking illustration of this phenomenon.

> A blind man is standing at the corner of a busy intersection in Miami Beach [a community known for its large number of Jewish residents]. He is having difficulty in crossing the street. A woman comes by and asks if he would like some help. "Det vood be vunderful," he replies. She starts leading him across the street. "It's so nice you should help me," the man says, "I vonder if also I could esk you a qvestion?" "Certainly," the woman replies. "Could you look at my socks and tell me if dey metch?" "Well, since you ask, one of them is yellow and one of them is blue." "Un-hunh, end vot about my pents, do dey metch my jecket?" "Well, actually, you're wearing purple pants and your jacket is green." "Uh, and vot about my tie? Does it metch either de pents or de jecket?" "Well, your tie is orange with pink polka-dots." By now, the two have safely crossed the street. The man says, "I vont to tenk you not only for helping me cross de street but also for enswering all my qvestions." "Oh, that's all right. I was glad to do it. But there is one more thing, as long as we're talking." "Yeah? Vot's det?" "You can drop the accent, you're a shvartzer."

To understand the joke, one has to know that *shvartzer* is the Yiddish word for black (Rosten 1970:381). In some versions of this joke, the man explains that he was adopted and blind from birth. In any case, the joke suggests that individuals tend to assimilate the identity features of the group surrounding them. Interestingly enough, the woman does not speak with a Jewish accent, although presumably from her use of the word *shvartzer*, she is Jewish. This may be to provide a marked contrast to the pronounced Jewish accent of the man, but it may also once again point to the Jew's attempt to conceal his identity. Also significant is the preoccupation with color in the joke's dialogue. It is as if to emphasize that the man is "color-blind," color being an older word in the south for blacks.

Identification of strangers

Members of groups are often anxious to find or rather identify strangers as members of their group. In most parts of the world with kinship-centered, social organization, two "strangers" meeting may establish some kind of relationship through kinship ties. In modern Euro-American society, two "strangers" will commonly play a variation of "Do you know?" until they find some person they both know—even if it is only a friend of a friend of a friend. A Jew may be curious to know whether a new acquaintance is Jewish or not and it is not always easy to determine such identity from physical appearance alone. One bit of folklore used in such a situation involves the first individual asking the second if he is a M.O.T., an acronym for "Member of the Tribe." Presumably, the inquirer would not even ask the question unless he were reasonably certain that the person interrogated was Jewish, as it might be embarrassing to explain what M.O.T. was to a *goy* (cf. Lyman & Douglass on "ethnic clues" (1973:362)). Incidentally, one very common event which often occurs after two Jews meet for the first time is that they begin swapping Jewish jokes, another reminder of the crucial importance of folklore in defining and confirming identity.

Another example of an acronymic, identity-search device is provided by a ritual taught to pledges of the Delta Chi fraternity. If a member of this national fraternity has reason to think that he has met a "brother," he will initiate a series of questions and responses as follows:

Do you know Kimball?
E. L. Kimball, the insurance salesman?
L. E. Kimball's my friend's name.
Tall man, with a dark beard?
A rather tall man.

Can't be my friend Kimball.
He doesn't know you.
I don't know him.

The first letters in each of the set sentences spell out the name of the fraternity: Delta Chi. Interestingly enough, the dialogue suggests that the two individuals carrying out the conversation do *not* have a friend in common. Of course, if the suspected brother doesn't give the correct response to the initial inquiry "Do you know Kimball?" then the questioner would not say anything further. As soon as the second sentence of this secret formula is uttered, the common identity is revealed and the remainder of the dialogue is simply an affirmation of the group's solidarity.

Folklorist W. Edson Richmond of Indiana University reported (personal communication) a variant of the above fraternity recognition formula:

Do you know Kimball?
E. A. Kimball, the insurance man?
L. A. Kimball is the man I know.
Tall man with a dark beard?
A rather tall man, but he has no beard.

Can't be the man I know.
He is a very fine fellow.
I should like to meet your friend.

Professor Richmond indicated that the ritual was not taught to pledges but only to fully initiated members of the fraternity.

The attempt to locate other members of one's identity group may involve costume or dress rather than verbal means. For example, the homosexual community has an elaborate dress code. In contrast to the standard preeminence of the right hand (Hertz

1960), we find a left-right distinction in which left is aggressive and dominant with right being passive, submissive. Thus, a homosexual may wear one ear-ring or one nose-post, but what is critical is whether it is worn in the left or right ear or nostril. Correspondingly, keys hanging off the belt to the left or right, or a handkerchief hanging out from a left or right pocket also advertise sexual availability and preference (Fischer 1977:7). Dominant versus passive refers, of course, to being an active or passive partner (Rodgers 1972:17, 146) in the performance of anal intercourse.

There are numerous other examples of the connection between costume and identity. For example, in Moravian Slovakia, single girls typically wore their hair in a simple braid, in contrast to married women who wore their hair in two braids wrapped around a pad or frame with a "marriage-cap" over their bound-up hair. Unwed mothers were not allowed to wear the hanging braid which signified virginity but were obliged to wear their hair in the married fashion (Bogatyrev 1971:72–73). In urban America, *The Official Preppy Handbook*, a trendy bestseller which purports to describe the distinctive features of elite young men and women (who attended select prep [preparatory] secondary schools), devotes an extensive section (1980:119–156) to "Dressing the Part," which ranges from jeans and T-shirts to blue blazer jackets and "Rules for the Monogramming of Men's Shirts." This form of identity, at least superficially, is available to anyone with the funds necessary to purchase the accouterments prescribed. As Klapp observes, "It is now true, in our land of ambiguous identity, that anyone may adopt almost any status symbol which he can afford. He may have his Cadillac, the new look of fashion, the fashionable address, the fancy letterhead. He announces and maintains any identity that he can get away with" (1969:31). What we have here is the possibility of "instant identity," which is not far removed from the whole notion of instant gratification. In the same way, joining new cults and crusades provides a relatively quick means of acquiring a new identity (Klapp 1969:137, 309).

One reason why individuals are so anxious to acquire a new identity (and why there are so many academic symposia devoted to identity) is the fear of being lost in the crowd or being just a number or nonentity. Identification or ID, as it is called for short, tends to reduce the individual to a number. Forms to be filled out for bureaucratic purposes invariably demand a host of numbers: date of birth, social-security number, passport number, employment number, telephone number, home address (which often includes a postal zip-code number), bank-account number, automobile-license-plate number, credit-card number. No doubt, one of the most gruesome forms of the substitution of numbers for personal identity were the concentration-camp numbers which survivors still bear, now often as a badge which is a witness to their survival.

Man and numbers

The tendency to reduce man to numbers is perhaps a separate topic. But it is curious that in the western world-view, both time and space can be expressed in numerical terms. Geographic locations may be particularized in latitude and longitude. Time can be stated in words, but typically it is in numbers. One can say that it is mid-afternoon or that it is 3.30. Digital clocks and watches have further reduced the representation of time to numbers. Similarly, the date, when put on paperwork forms, could include the name of the month spelled out or its abbreviation, but, more often than not, the month is indicated by a number. Women are commonly perceived by men in terms of such folk measurements as bust, waist, and hips (36, 26, 36) or of ranking women on a beauty scale from one to ten, ten being the highest score.

One becomes increasingly aware of the importance of what has been termed man's "paper identity" (Schachtel 1961:120). One cannot prove that one has been born by just appearing before an official; one must present a birth certificate! Without the proper identity or identification cards, one cannot cash checks or be admitted to various activities. (In cashing checks in the United States, the store cashier usually writes one's driver's license number and a credit-card number on the check). When a customer enters a crowded and popular bakery or other shop, he may be asked to take a number. When his number is called, he is served. In American folk speech, to have someone's number is to know the hidden truth about another individual or to have classified or identified that individual. Also one speaks of doing things "by the numbers," that is, doing things according to the rules (deriving presumably from Army drilling slang). One hopes that one will *amount* to something, that one's contribution will *count*, preferably before one's *number* is up!

Many academic disciplines indulge in number worship, and folklore is no exception. Folklorists are wont to speak of tale type numbers—Cinderella is Aarne-Thompson tale type 510A—as well as motif numbers, for example, H 36.1, Slipper test, refers to the establishment of the heroine's identity through the fitting of the slipper. But, once again, folklore offers a comment, perhaps an antidote, to this tendency, specifically criticizing the absurdity of attempting to reduce folk-tales (or anything else) to numbers.

At a joke-tellers' convention, a man went up to the podium and said, "37." Everyone laughed. "45." Again, everyone roared. "51." Once more, the audience laughed. He sat down and another man took his place. "28," he said. The audience was silent. "74." Again, total silence. "62." Nothing. The man returned sadly to his seat. The person sitting next to him tried to console him: "It's not the joke, but the way you tell it." (In other versions, "Some can tell 'em and some can't.")

In another joke of this type, at the same convention, a person gets up and says "22." Everyone laughs. "93." Everyone laughs. "48." Again, everyone laughs, but this time one individual in the audience continues to laugh uproariously, rolling in the aisles, long after everyone else has stopped. The person sitting next to him looks curiously at the laughing individual, who responds by explaining, "I hadn't heard that one before."

So alienated members of urban societies who live and die by the numbers have their folklore too and in that folklore they may find their identity reflected. Not only does folklore serve as a kind of autobiographical ethnography, a mirror made by the people themselves, which reflects a group's identity, but it also represents valuable data which is relatively free from the outside observer's bias. Students of social identity have been anxious to minimize the interpretive distortion of social scientists, who cannot ever be said to be truly non-ethnocentric and bias-free (Zavalloni 1973:81).

Folklore data, which exists before the investigator arrives on the scene, avoids the difficulties of administering a "Who am I?" questionnaire, which is an *a priori* document made up by the investigators, not the people being studied. Folklore thus offers social scientists an unobtrusive technique for the gathering of information about identity. Folklore gives a view of a people from the inside-out rather than from the outside-in. There may well be distortion in folkloristic data, but at least it is distortion introduced by the people themselves, instead of the would-be objective, social scientist.

It is important to recognize that folklore is not simply a way of obtaining available data about identity for social scientists. It is actually one of the principal means by which an individual and a group discovers or establishes his or its identity. Let me conclude with one final example to illustrate just how important folklore is to the nature of human identity. As man fears becoming more and more like a machine, he also worries about machines becoming more and more human. Will robots and computers ever do away with the need for humans? The folk have an answer:

> A super computer is built and all the world's knowledge is programmed into it. A gathering of top scientists punch in the question: "Will the computer ever replace man?" Clickity, click, whir, whir, and the computer lights flash on and off. Finally, a small print-out emerges saying, "That reminds me of a story."

BIBLIOGRAPHY

Balfour, Henry. 1924. The Geography of Foklore. *Folk-Lore*, 35:16–25.

Barth, Fredrik (ed.). 1969. *Ethnic Groups and Boundaries*. Boston: Little, Brown.

Bauman, Richard. 1971. Differential Identity and the Social Base of Folklore. *Journal of American Folklore*, 85:31–41.

Bausinger, Hermann. 1977. Zur kulturalen Dimension von Identität. *Zeitschrift für Volkskunde*, 73:210–215.

Benoist, J. M. (ed.). 1977. *L'identité*. Seminaire interdisciplinaire dirigé par Claude Lévi-Strauss, professeur au Collège de France 1974–1975. Paris: Bernard Grasset.

Bergen, Fanny D. 1900. Fly-Leaf Rhymes and Decorations. *New England Magazine*, 23: 505–511.

Birnbach, Lisa (ed.). 1980. *The Official Preppy Handbook*. New York: Workman.

Bogatyrev, Petr. 1971. *The Functions of Folk Costume in Moravian Slovakia*. The Hague: Mouton.

Clark, Robert T., Jr. 1969. *Herder: His Life and Thought*. Berkeley and Los Angeles: University of California Press.

Dashefsky, Arnold. 1972. And the Search Goes On: The Meaning of Religio-Ethnic Identity and Identification. *Sociological Analysis*, 33:239–245.

———. 1975. Theoretical Frameworks in the Study of Ethnic Identity: Toward a Social Psychology of Ethnicity. *Ethnicity*, 2:10–18.

De Levita, David J. 1965. *The Concept of Identity*. New York: Basic Books.

De Vos, George. 1975. Ethnic Pluralism: Conflict and Accommodation. In George De Vos & Lola Romanucci-Ross (eds.), *Ethnic Identity: Cultural Continuities and Change*, pp. 5–41. Palo Alto: Mayfield Publishing Company.

Dorson, Richard. 1960. Jewish-American Dialect Stories on Tape. In Raphael Patai, Francis Lee Utley & Dov Noy (eds.), *Studies in Biblical and Jewish Folklore*, pp. 111–174. Indiana University Folklore Series No. 13. Bloomington: Indiana University Press.

Dundes, Alan. 1971. A Study of Ethnic Slurs: The Jew and the Polack in the United States. *Journal of American Folklore*, 84:186–203.

———. 1973. *Mother Wit from the Laughing Barrel: Readings in the Interpretation of Afro-American Folklore*. Englewood Cliffs: Prentice-Hall.

———. 1975. Slurs International: Folk Comparisons of Ethnicity and National Character. *Southern Folklore Quarterly*, 39:15–38.

———. 1980. *Interpreting Folklore*. Bloomington: Indiana University Press.

———. 1981. Life Is Like a Chicken-coop Ladder: A Study of German National Character through Folklore. *Journal of Psychoanalytic Anthropology*, 4:265–364.

Dundes, Alan & Falassi, Alessandro. 1975. *La Terra in Piazza: An Interpretation of the Palio of Siena*. Berkeley and Los Angeles: University of California Press.

Dundes, Alan & Pagter, Carl R. 1975. *Urban Folklore from the Paperwork Empire*. Austin: American Folklore Society.

Eidheim, Harald. 1969. When Ethnic Identity Is a Social Stigma. In Fredrik Barth (ed.), *Ethnic Groups and Boundaries*, pp. 39–57. Boston: Little, Brown.

Ergang, Robert. 1931. *Herder and the Foundations of German Nationalism*. New York: Columbia University Press.

Erikson, Erik H. 1956. The Problem of Ego Identity. *Journal of the American Psychoanalytic Association*, 4:56–121.

———. 1963. *Childhood and Society*. 2nd ed. New York: Norton.

————. 1968. *Identity: Youth and Crisis*. New York: Norton.

————. 1980. *Identity and the Life Cycle*. New York: Norton.

Fischer, Hal. 1977. *Gay Semiotics: A Photographic Study of Visual Coding among Homosexual Men*. San Francisco: NFS Press.

Fullerton, George Stuart. 1890. *On Sameness and Identity*. Philadelphia: University of Pennsylvania Press.

Gilman, Sander L. 1986. *Jewish Self-Hatred: Anti-Semitism and the Hidden Language of the Jews*. Baltimore: The Johns Hopkins University Press.

Greenacre, Phyllis. 1958. Early Physical Determinants in the Development of the Sense of Identity. *Journal of the American Psychoanalytic Association*, 6:612–627.

Handelman, Don. 1977. The Organization of Ethnicity. *Ethnic Groups*, 1:187–200.

Hasluck, Margaret. 1949. Oedipus Rex in Albania. *Folklore*, 60:340–348.

Hertz, Robert. 1960. *Death and the Right Hand*. London: Cohen & West.

Honko, Lauri. 1980. Upptäckten av folkdiktning och nationell identitet i Finland. *Tradisjon*, 10:33–51.

————. 1982. Folktradition och identitet. In Aili Nenola-Kallio (ed.), *Folktradition och regional identitet i Norden*, pp. 11–23. Åbo: NIF.

————. 1988. *Tradition and Cultural Identity*. Turku: NIF.

Hooper, Michael. 1976. The Structure and Measurement of Social Identity. *Public Opinion Quarterly*, 40:154–164.

Hultkrantz, Åke. 1960. *General Ethnological Concepts*. Copenhagen: Rosenkilde & Bagger.

Hume, David. 1911. *A Treatise of Human Nature*, Vol. I. London: J. M. Dent.

Isaacs, Harold R. 1975. Basic Group Identity: The Idols of the Tribe. In Nathan Glazer & Daniel P. Moynihan (eds.), *Ethnicity: Theory and Experience*, pp. 29–52. Cambridge: Harvard University Press.

Isajiw, Wsevolod W. 1974. Definitions of Ethnicity. *Ethnicity*, 1:111–124.

Joyce, James. 1964. *A Portrait of the Artist as a Young Man*. New York: Penguin.

Kamenetsky, Christa. 1974. Folklore Revival in Slovenia: A Quest for Cultural Identity. *Library Journal*, 99:1441–1445.

Kardiner, Abram & Ovesey, Lionel. 1962. *The Mark of Oppression: Explorations in the Personality of the American Negro*. Cleveland: Meridian Books.

Kastersztein, Joseph. 1981. Aspects psychosociaux de l'identité. *Social Science Information*, 20:95–109.

Klapp, Orrin E. 1969. *Collective Search for Identity*. New York: Holt, Rinehart & Winston.

Kuhn, Manford H. & McPartland, Thomas S. 1954. An Empirical Investigation of Self-Attitudes. *American Sociological Review*, 19:68–76.

Levine, Lawrence W. 1977. *Black Culture and Black Consciousness: Afro-American Folk Thought from Slavery to Freedom.* New York: Oxford University Press.

Lewin, Kurt. 1941. Self-Hatred among Jews. *Contemporary Jewish Record*, 4:219–232.

Limón, José E. 1977. Agringado Joking in Texas Mexican Society: Folklore and Differential Identity. *New Scholar*, 6:33–50.

Locke, John. 1959. *An Essay concerning Human Understanding*, Vol. I. New York: Dover.

Luckmann, Thomas. 1979. Personal Identity as an Evolutionary and Historical Problem. In M. von Cranach, K. Foppa, W. Lepenies and D. Ploog (eds.), *Human Ethology: Claims and Limits of a New Discipline*, pp. 56–74. Cambridge: Cambridge University Press.

Lyman, Stanford M. & Douglass, William A. 1973. Ethnicity: Strategies of Collective and Individual Impression Management. *Social Research*, 40:344–365.

McCartney, Eugene S. 1922. Sex Determination and Sex Control in Antiquity. *American Journal of Philology*, 43:62–70.

Mead, Margaret. 1958 *Israel and Problems of Identity*. Herzl Institute Pamphlets 3. New York: Theodor Herzl Foundation.

N'Diaye, Alphonse Raphaël. 1980. Les traditions orales et la quête de l'identité culturelle. *Présence Africaine*, 114:3–17.

Noonan, Harold W. 1980. *Objects and Identity: An Examination of the Relative Identity Thesis and Its Consequences*. The Hague: Martinus Nijhoff.

Oliveira, Roberto Cardoso de. 1976. *Identidade, Etnia e Estrutura Social*. São Paulo: Livraria Pioneira Editora.

Propp, Vladimir. 1968. *Morphology of the Folktale*. Austin: University of Texas Press.

Rodgers, Bruce, 1972. *The Queens' Vernacular: A Gay Lexicon*. San Francisco: Straight Arrow Books.

Rosten, Leo. 1970. *The Joys of Yiddish*. New York: Pocket Books.

Royce, Anya Peterson. 1982. *Ethnic Identity: Strategies of Diversity*. Bloomington: Indiana University Press.

Rubenfine, David L. 1958. Problems of Identity. *Journal of the American Psychoanalytic Association*, 6:131–142.

Sarbin, Theodore R. & Karl E. Scheibe, (eds.). 1983. *Studies in Social Identity* New York: Praeger.

Schachtel, Ernest G. 1961. On Alienated Concepts of Identity. *American Journal of Psychoanalysis*, 21:120–127.

Schmidt, Gerold. 1976. Identität: Gebrauch und Geschichte eines modernen Begriffs. *Muttersprache*, 86:333–354.

Spicer, Edward H. 1971. Persistent Cultural Systems: A Comparative Study of Identity Systems That Can Adapt to Contrasting Environments. *Science*, 174, no. 4011:795–800.

Taboada-Leonetti, Isabelle. 1981. Identité individuelle, identité collective. *Social Science Information*, 20:137–167.

Tap, Pierre (ed.). 1980. *Identités collectives et changements sociaux*. Toulouse: Privat.

Twain, Mark. 1948. *The Adventures of Huckleberry Finn*. New York: Holt, Rinehart & Winston.

Vikis-Freibergs, Vaira. 1975. Echoes of the *Dainas* and the Search for Identity in Contemporary Latvian Poetry. *Journal of Baltic Studies*, 6:17–29.

Weber, Max. 1968. *Economy and Society*, Vol. I. New York: Bedminster Press.

Wilder, Thornton. 1938. *Our Town*. New York: Coward McCann.

Zavalloni, Marisa. 1973. Social Identity: Perspectives and Prospects. *Social Science Information*, 12 (3):65–91.

The Fabrication of Fakelore

In a 1950 issue of a semi-popular periodical, *American Mercury*, folklorist Richard M. Dorson coined the neologism 'fakelore.' In his brief essay entitled "Folklore and Fake Lore" (two words which were later to become one), Dorson began a lifelong battle to promote the scientific study of folklore and to attack fake folklore or fakelore. He was to return to this distinction many times, as for example, in the article "Fakelore" published in 1969, and in *Folklore and Fakelore: Essays toward a Discipline of Folk Studies* which appeared in 1976.

What exactly did Dorson mean by the term fakelore? "Fakelore is the presentation of spurious and synthetic writings under the claim that they are genuine folklore. These productions are not collected in the field but are rewritten from earlier literary and journalistic sources in an endless chain of regurgitation, or they may even be made out of whole cloth, as in the case of several of the 'folk heroes' written up in the image of Paul Bunyan, who had at least some trickle of oral tradition at the beginning of his literary exploitation."[1]

Dorson's repeated excoriations of fakelore as well as of those who produced it often bordered on near-manic acerbic expressions of vitriol. He seemingly never tired of criticizing any "synthetic product claiming to be authentic oral tradition but actually tailored for mass edification" and he even charged that "the authors, editors, and publishers had misled and gulled the public."[2]

Dorson singled out in particular the cycle of Paul Bunyan stories, contending "there is no body of Paul Bunyan legends."[3] For Dorson, Paul Bunyan epitomized his conception of fakelore. Most of the reported Bunyan adventures could be shown to have been composed by various identifiable writers, one of whom issued such stories as part of a commercial advertising campaign for the Red River Lumber Company.[4] Although there may well have been an initial authentic "trickle of oral tradition" as Dorson felicitously phrased it, concerning Paul Bunyan, certainly the vast majority of published Paul Bunyan stories never enjoyed oral circulation, though to be sure, the extent of the "trickle" continues to be hotly debated.[5]

Another frequent object of Dorson's scorn was the series of "treasuries" of folklore compiled by Benjamin Botkin. Botkin, who published his enormously popular *Treasury of American Folklore* in 1944, tended to rely principally upon printed, written sources, and he felt free to rewrite the materials for the wider audience which his treasuries targeted. Dorson in commenting upon Botkin's apparent refusal to leave the library likened him to "the dude fisherman who buys his catch at the market."[6]

It should be made clear that Dorson was not criticizing poets and men of letters who used genuine folklore as the source or inspiration for literary prose and poetry. For there is a long and honored tradition of literature based upon or derived from oral tradition. What Dorson was objecting to was the particular case in which an individual first fabricated material and then had the audacity to claim that it was pure, unadulterated oral folklore. For Dorson, there was an undeniable dichotomy between folklore (which was good) and fakelore (which was evil).

Fakelore should also be distinguished from the concepts of survival and revival. Survival implies a continuity of tradition, no matter how diminished or altered in form an item of folklore might be. Revival suggests discontinuity, a break in the tradition. It refers to a conscious decision to resuscitate an item of folklore that flourished in the past. Fakelore, in contrast, never existed at all—at least in the form presented.

Although it is perfectly understandable why fakelore to purist, academic folklorists represents the enemy, insofar as it attempts to improve upon or even replace bona fide folklore, the existence of fakelore has been intricately and inseparably involved with the study of folklore from its very beginnings at the end of the eighteenth century. Dorson, despite his historical turn of mind, seems not to have seen the connection between the concept of fakelore, the articulation of which gave him such justified pride, and the famous or rather infamous Ossian poems published in the 1760s by James Macpherson, the Grimms' *Kinder- und Hausmärchen* of 1812 and 1815, and the publication of the Finnish national epic, the *Kalevala*, in 1835.

James Macpherson (1736–1796) published *Fragments of Ancient Poetry Collected in the Highlands of Scotland and Translated from the Gaelic or Erse Language* in 1760. Then followed *Fingal: An Ancient Epic Poem* in 1762, and *Temora* in 1763. These works were brought together and published in *Poems of Ossian* in 1765, the same year Bishop Percy's *Reliques of Ancient English Poetry* appeared. The authenticity of these allegedly traditional poems was challenged soon after their publication. Samuel Johnson, after some "field" investigation, claimed in *Journey to the Western Islands* in 1775 that Macpherson had found only fragments of ancient poems and that he himself had composed most of the poetry he presented as coming from tradition.[7] Scottish philosopher David Hume (1711–1776) was one of many who became embroiled in the Ossian controversy. He even wrote a tract "Of the Authenticity of Ossian's Poems" in which he expressed his doubts,[8] although for various personal and political reasons the essay was not published until many years later in 1846.[9] In a letter of 1763 addressed to the Reverend Hugh Blair who had written a *Critical Dissertation on the Poems of Ossian* the same year in which he defended Macpherson against charges of forgery and the like, Hume asked for proof rather than faith. "These proofs must not be arguments, but testimonies"[10] and these testimonies should include oral tradition. Hume's insistence upon verifiable oral sources sounds remarkably modern.[11]

A close, detailed study of the possible Gaelic sources of Macpherson's Ossian reveals that although he tapped a genuine stream of Scottish Highland oral tradition, he was not very faithful to it. His poetic license coupled with apparent misunderstanding of Gaelic dialect words led to a literary mishmash quite far removed from oral style.[12] Macpherson combined different versions of individual ballads to produce composite texts and then felt free to add or delete what he pleased. A dramatic ballad story becomes "jerky and incoherent" in Macpherson's retelling; in another instance "Macpherson may be said to adapt his sources with some ingenuity, but in so doing he loses much of the story. The representation becomes blurred . . . at times indeed, the course of the story becomes hard to follow. In this telling the tale has lost its tragedy, its pathos, its dignity, and practically all its meaning."[13] The author of the most comprehensive study of Ossian's sources remarks, "Here, as elsewhere in Macpherson's work, it is not easy to assess what is disingenuous and what is written in good faith and bad judgment."[14]

With respect to good faith, it appears that Macpherson did collect bits and pieces from oral tradition, but he assumed they were the remnants of an ancient epic tradition and accordingly did his best to put them into a unified, orderly arrangement.[15] Some of his sources were oral fragments; some were manuscript materials.[16] However, as one commentator has observed, "In his preface and introductory dissertation Macpherson refrained from clearly explaining to the public that his epic had, as his literary friends very well knew, been formed out of fragments; nay, in one passage, he spoke of laying the work before his readers as he had found it."[17] There is evidence that Macpherson did present the "originals" of his field notes to his publishers during several months of 1762 in order for sceptics to examine them if they so wished.[18] Nevertheless, Macpherson did not publish the original texts in full.

If fakelore is "the presentation of spurious and synthetic writings under the claim that they are genuine folklore," then it would seem that Macpherson's Ossian may qualify as one of the first documented cases of fakelore. Yet it is also true that this fakelore proved to have enormous influence. Regardless of whether Ossian was fakelore or folklore, it stimulated an interest in the poetry of the common man throughout Europe. Eighteenth century neo-classicism had pointed exclusively towards the classical models of ancient Greece and Rome. The possibility of eliciting oral poetry from the Scottish Highlands meant that epic poetry could come not just from the ancients, but also from modern, untutored peasants. The glorification of the noble savage sprang from the same source. And so came the beginnings of a curious combination of romanticism, primitivism, and nationalism which were to prevail in the nineteenth century and which were to accompany if not provide the important impetus for the rise of folkloristics as a serious, academic pursuit.

In considering the foundings of folkloristics, one cannot fail to think of the Grimm brothers. They are generally credited as being two of the pioneering figures in the study of folklore. Their collections and publication of German folklore sparked a virtual intellectual revolution, spurring would-be folklorists in many countries to gather their own local traditions. In a circular dated 1815, Jakob Grimm (1785–1863) gave specific suggestions as to how to collect oral traditions. He included the following: "One should, above all, be concerned with conceiving these items faithfully and correctly from the mouth of the narrators, without make-up and addition, where possible in and with their proper words. . . ." Earlier, in the 1812 preface to the first volume of the *Kinder- und Hausmärchen*, the Grimms made such claims as "we have endeavored to present these fairy-tales as purely as possible. . . . No circumstance has been added, embellished or changed. . . ." Yet the Grimms did not practice what they preached. So the version of the Grimm tale number 21, Aschenputtel (Cinderella) which appeared in 1812, was by the edition of 1819, seven years later, already expanded and reworked in the light of three versions from Hesse. The Grimms, especially Wilhelm, began to combine versions into composite texts, feeling free to fill in details or re-tell tales more "simply and purely" than in the originals.

An in-depth study of the hallowed Grimm folktale canon reveals many such discrepancies.[19] Moreover, there is evidence not only that the Grimms doctored the tales they purportedly collected directly from the lips of peasants, but that they also falsified informant data. They said, for example, that Dorothea Viehmann was an ideal storyteller, a German peasant who told from memory ancient Hessian tales, whereas actually they knew very well that she was an educated, literate middle-class woman whose first language was French, not German.[20] The Grimms' offenses included disguising their actual sources and even destroying all of their original field notes. According to Ellis,[21] the notes were destroyed "to make sure that no one would know that they had in fact extensively elaborated and rewritten all their source material, changing form and content at will, and doubling and sometimes tripling the length of a text." The conclusion is "The Grimms wanted to create a German national monument while pretending that they had merely discovered it; and later on, no one wanted to seem to tear it down."[22] It is true that folklorists have tended on the whole to gloss over these facts, preferring instead to continue to extol the Grimms as shining exemplars of folklore scholarship.

It does seem almost sacrilegious to label the Grimms' celebrated *Kinder- und Hausmärchen* as fakelore, but to the extent that oral materials are re-written, embellished and elaborated, and then presented as if they were pure, authentic oral tradition, we do indeed have a prima facie case of fakelore. One can legitimately argue that both Macpherson and the Grimms were important in the development of folkloristics in terms of what they claimed they had accomplished, namely, collecting folklore from peasants in their own words—regardless of what liberties they may have taken with these oral materials.

A few years after the appearance of the Grimms' tales, in the late 1820s, Elias Lönnrot (1802–1884), a young doctor, began carrying out fieldwork to collect folk poetry, especially from Finnish Karelia. In 1831, Lönnrot, with a small group of like-minded friends, established the Finnish Literature Society which has ever since proven to be a major inspiration in the amassing and study of Finnish folklore. In the early 1830s, Lönnrot continued his fieldtrips, but also began thinking about arranging the different songs and placing them in some kind of logical narrating order. In 1835, he published the first edition of the *Kalevala*. It struck a remarkably responsive chord in Finnish national consciousness and was hailed as an epic which had existed since time immemorial. Lönnrot was praised for having successfully restored its fragmentary elements into its original full form. Lönnrot and other devoted students of Finnish tradition collected additional verses. In 1849, he published a revised edition. Whereas the first 1835 edition contained 32 poems and 5,052 lines, the 1849 edition included some 50 poems and 22, 795 lines. It is not altogether clear just how many Finns ever regarded the *Kalevala* as an authentic oral epic.

Some understood it was Lönnrot who had put together different individual, discrete songs, but they assumed that the individual songs at least were genuine oral tradition. As William Wilson observes, "In actual fact, not only is the *Kalevala* a composite epic, so also are the poems in it composite poems; no one song has ever been recited by the people the way it appears in the *Kalevala*."[23]

The *Kalevala* would seem to be a classic example of fakelore. It involves literary embellishment and re-writing of what may or may not have been an original oral narrative plot. Yet leading Finnish folklorists actually defended the idea that the *Kalevala* should count as a legitimate national folk epic. No less a figure than Kaarle Krohn, first university professor of folklore at the University of Helsinki—he began teaching in 1888 and he was appointed to the first permanent chair of Finnish and Comparative Folklore in 1908—took such a position. Krohn, one of the founders of the famous Folklore Fellows, an international group of scholars formed in 1907 and dedicated to uplifting the standards of folkloristics, actually claimed that Lönnrot, despite his university education, could be considered as a kind of folk poet.[24] Krohn, of course, knew better, and eventually admitted that although the *Kalevala* might always be the cornerstone of Finnish literature, it was useless for scientific studies inasmuch as Lönnrot's hand had frequently changed the original order.[25] Finnish folklorist Martti Haavio once remarked that it was Krohn who had taught him that "the *Kalevala* frankly and openly speaking, is a clear counterfeit."[26] The problem was that although folklorists knew very well that the "*Kalevala* is not regular folklore," as Haavio wrote in 1954,[27] the Finnish people, including many intellectuals, preferred instead to believe that the *Kalevala* was a genuine folk epic.[28]

The forces of romanticism and nationalism were—and are—so powerful in Finald that what the people *believed* was—and is—more important than what was true. So if the Finnish people believe the *Kalevala* is a folk epic, it does little good for Finnish (and foreign) folklorists to point out that the *Kalevala* is fakelore. It might be noted en passant that the Estonians have much the same determined nationalistic sentiments about their so-called national epic, the *Kalevipoeg*, inspired in part by (envy of) the Finnish *Kalevala*, even though its connection with authentic oral tradition is even less likely.[29]

Folklorists cannot prevent people from believing that fakelore is folklore. In considering the American case of Paul Bunyan, we can observe the same reasoning. One of the popularizers criticized by Dorson responded, "Well, if the American public thinks Paul Bunyan is a folk hero, then we have to treat him as one."[30] It becomes strictly an argument by origins to insist that Paul Bunyan's exploits are fakelore. Furthermore there remains the distinct possibility that Paul Bunyan might be Canadian rather than American in genesis.[31] It is only scholarly folklorists who are concerned with oral pedigrees. I suspect that probably most Americans do consider Paul Bunyan as an authentic American folk hero (except the relatively small number who may have read Dorson's objections). The fact that dozens of Paul Bunyan statues adorn the American landscape in front of lodges and highway restaurants attests to the extent to which Paul Bunyan has entered the American consciousness. To Dorson's extreme annoyance, the very dust jacket of his *American Folklore and the Historian*, a selection of essays, the first one being "Fakelore," prominently displayed a picture of Paul Bunyan. Presses rarely consult authors about book jacket design, but it surely demonstrated the strength of national popular culture to have a pictorial representation of Paul Bunyan with his huge axe resting on his shoulder on the front cover of a book written by a man who devoted considerable time and energy during his long and illustrious academic career to proving that Paul Bunyan was fakelore!

We can only surmise that perhaps oral tradition is not enough. In Scotland, in Germany, in Finland, and in twentieth-century America, there was indisputably a need to invent tradition. And not just to invent tradition, but to label it tradition! Macpherson claimed that Ossian was genuine oral poetry; the Grimms maintained that they had recorded and presented pure oral tradition; Lönnrot honestly felt he was only reconstructing or restoring an authentic, ancient Finnish epic; and perhaps the various authors of Paul Bunyan stories felt they were simply embroidering or expanding the saga of a true American folk figure.

Helped by the perspective of hindsight, we can discern a common element in these apparently disparate instances of fakelore. In all cases, the country in question was suffering from a severe case of an inferiority complex—if one can appropriately speak of an entire country being affected by such a complex. Scotland, for example, in the late eighteenth century was frequently the subject of humor and abuse by the English.[32] Hume, himself a Scot, had this to say about Scottish Highlanders in a letter of March 18, 1776, addressed to Edward Gibbon: "I see you entertain a great doubt with regard to the authenticity of the Poems of Ossian. You are certainly right in so doing. It is, indeed, strange, that any men of Sense could have imagin'd it possible, that above twenty thousand Verses, along with numberless historical Facts, could have been preserved by oral Tradition during fifty Generations, by the rudest, perhaps of all European Nations; the most necessitous, the most turbulent, and the most unsettled,"[33] a passage echoed verbatim in his essay on the authenticity of Ossian's poems.[34] Although Hume was anxious to discover a worthy Scottish poet to demonstrate Scottish national greatness, he felt that Scotsmen should refrain from writing in their spoken national language of Scottish Gaelic, using standard English instead.[35] Here is a critical paradox inherent in the development of folkloristics everywhere and related to strong, unresolved feelings of ambivalence on the part of intellectuals towards the folk and towards folklore. On the one hand, the folk are all too common, the *vulgus in populo*. In Hume's words, the folk is rude. The folk is a backward, illiterate segment of the population of which elitist intellectuals are ashamed. On the other hand, the folk represents the glorified, romanticized remnants of a national patrimony which is something for zealous intellectuals to celebrate. So Hume seeks a national Scottish poet, but he deprecates the rude Scottish Highlanders and he repudiates Scottish Gaelic in favor of English. The same situation applies in most countries. Intellectuals were both embarrassed by and proud of their folk and folklore. Inferiority breeds superiority! Trevor-Roper summarizes how Macpherson's Ossian put Scottish Highlanders on the map: "Previously despised alike by the Lowland Scots, as disorderly savages, and by the Irish as their unlettered poor kinsmen, they were now celebrated throughout Europe as a *Kulturvolk* which, when England and Ireland had been sunk in primitive barbarism, had produced an epic poet of exquisite refinement and sensibility."[36]

A comparable scene prevailed in pre-Grimm Germany. "Whatever the reasons, however, Germany in the mid-eighteenth century was culturally backward compared to its neighbors, and consequently afflicted by a national cultural inferiority complex. . . . Germany at this time looked enviously at the culture of its neighbors; even so great a German patriot and national hero as Frederick the Great, king of Prussia, despised the German language, spoke and wrote in French, and was so convinced of the great superiority of French literature and culture generally than even when Mozart and Goethe arrived on the scene, he thought little of them."[37]

In Finland, Finns were for several centuries under the rule and cultural domination of the Swedes, and as Wilson justly observes, "It was against this background of Swedification of Finnish culture that the stirrings of Finnish national consciousness first began to appear."[38] By the end of the eighteenth century, educated Finns spoke Swedish while the Finnish language was spoken only by peasants.[39]

Such parallels are too striking to be coincidental, and I would argue that Americans have long felt inferior to Europe in general and to England and France in particular. Even up to the beginning of the twentieth century, the elite, that is, the artists, writers, composers, went to live and study in Europe rather than remain in the United States. It was hard for citizens of the United States to forget that they lived in an area which was a former set of colonies. They continued to think of themselves as living in the "provinces" and they looked to the Old World for trend-setting fashions in art, music, and literature, not to mention cuisine and dress. Paul Bunyan reflected America's self-image: big and strong, but not very intelligent or refined. To some extent, that American self-image remains as "naive" American politicians feel outmanned and outmaneuvered by the more sophisticated leaders of European countries. The War of 1812 was inconclusive, although it did reveal the American resentment of England and its continuing struggle to be free of England's political and cultural domination. It was not really until World War I that America began to occupy a central position on the world stage of major powers.

In this context, it is no accident that Paul Bunyan stories began to emerge about the same time. While oral reports date from around the turn of the twentieth century,[40] Paul Bunyan first appeared in print in a feature article for the *Detroit Tribune* of July 25, 1910, with a small thirty-page booklet, *Introducing Mr. Paul Bunyan of Westwood Cal.* published in 1914.[41] Benjamin Botkin's bestseller anthology, *Treasury of American Folklore*, was first published in 1944, during World War II. Although Dorson castigates both the Paul Bunyan materials and Botkin's *Treasury* as fakelore—both involved the literary rehashing of oral materials coupled with the invention and addition of new (= untraditional) details—he failed to comment on the possible significance of the time of their appearance.

Fakelore apparently fills a national, psychic need: namely, to assert one's national identity, especially in a time of crisis, and to instill pride in that identity. Hobsbawm claims that "Where the old ways are alive, traditions need be neither revived nor invented."[42] It may be true that ideally folklore serves the cause of national identity cravings, but where folklore is deemed lacking or insufficient, individual creative writers imbued with nationalistic zeal have felt free to fill in that void. They do so by creating a national epic or national "folk" hero *ex nihilo* if necessary, or what is more usual, they embroider and inflate fragments of folklore into fakeloristic fabrications.

Fakelore, it should be observed, applies equally to non-verbal materials. Kilts and clan tartans are just as good examples of Scottish fakelore as Ossian.[43] The open air folk museums, so popular in Europe since the late nineteenth century, contain collocations of buildings moved from diverse original sites into one composite "village." Moreover, in each building, furnishings have often been added and the furnishings are not always from the original structure. Each room represents an analog to a composite text as well. And it is not just fakelore which is fabricated, but fake history, too. There are numerous instances of spurious historiographic reconstructions of "golden ages" of the past designed to shore up the self-respect of a given national or ethnic group.[44]

Folklorists have long realized the connection between national-ism and folklore,[45] but what has not been perceived is the possible relationship between feelings of national inferiority and the ten-dency to produce fakelore. If folklore is rooted in nationalism, I believe fakelore may be said to be rooted in feelings of national or cultural inferiority. As feelings of nationalism may be tied to feelings of cultural inferiority, so folklore may be linked with fakelore. Apparently, the feelings of inferiority are so strong as to compel some of the pioneering figures in folklore to alter drasti-cally the folklore they collected so as to "improve" it, thereby making it the intellectual equal of the classic literary heritages of what are deemed more advanced cultures. A folk in this light would be so anxious to prove its equality—or better yet, superi-ority—that its self-appointed representatives would take the re-sponsibility upon themselves to consciously manipulate or even fabricate materials to offer as proof.

In terms of the distinction between oral and literary conven-tions, these various patriotic early collectors of folklore typically imposed literary criteria upon oral materials. The end product was invariably a conscious, literary epic or tale, not an unself-conscious oral narrative. However, inasmuch as these well-inten-tioned revisionists claimed that the materials they presented were genuine folklore, they were guilty of fabricating fakelore.

We can now better understand why it is that certain small coun-tries suffering from poor self-images vis-à-vis other nations, for example, relatively small countries like Finland, Hungary, and Ireland, have been particularly active in collecting and studying folklore. And we can also see why certain smug countries suffering from superiority complexes vis-à-vis other nations—England and France—have been markedly less interested in collecting and studying their own folklore. (Both England and France have been involved in studying the folklore materials of their colonial posses-sions, but that was in part a reflection of a concern with how to better administer and control dependent peoples.) In this context, it also becomes clearer why Germany, depressed after its humiliat-ing defeat in World War I, turned to folklore to promote Nazi ide-ology.[46] Such ideology even impelled "scholars" to invent "anti-Semitic proverbs to support the Nazi drive to exterminate the

Jews,"[47] surely, one of the most insidious of all the documented instances of fakelore.

By placing fakelore into a larger historical and cultural perspective, we can observe that it is by no means confined to twentieth-century America. I believe Dorson was in error when he claimed, "There appears to be no close parallel in other nations to the fakelore issue in the United States."[48] Others have followed Dorson in assuming fakelore to be a twentieth-century phenomenon.[49] Fakelore may be found in eighteenth-century Scotland, nineteenth-century Germany and Finland, plus many, many other countries and periods. In Belgium, for example, we have the case of Charles De Coster (1827–1879) who revamped through bowdlerization and excessive emendation the Germanic Til Eulenspiegel cycle. After a preliminary *La Legende d'Ulenspiegel* appeared in 1867, a full-fledged edition appeared in 1869. Although most of the original earthy, bawdy character of Eulenspiegel has been eliminated, De Coster was acclaimed as a national poet, and some Flemish critics called his creation the "Flemish bible," remarking that it truly reflected the Flemish soul.[50] Similarly, in Switzerland, schoolmasters under the influence of nationalistic fervor composed supplementary "folksongs," while traditional marksmanship contests à la William Tell were ritually institutionalized to promote a heightened sense of Swiss national consciousness.[51]

If fakelore is an example of what Hobsbawm has termed "invented tradition," and if it is as pervasive as the above evidence indicates, how should the folklorist regard it? Dorson's counsel was to condemn it, but this seems somewhat futile. For one thing, fakelore can in theory become folklore. A composite text, however spuriously crafted, can go into oral tradition. (There is evidence, for example, that some of the Grimm versions of standard tale types have been collected from oral sources—from individuals who directly or indirectly learned their tales from the Grimm canon.) But on the whole, very little fakelore has become folklore. The fakelore produced through ideologically sponsored official propaganda campaigns, as for example, in China[52] or in the Soviet Union,[53] rarely enters oral tradition except in occasional parody form. The folk are much too wise to accept artificial concoctions as genuine folklore. Still, fakelore is fabricated for profit—the idea is to sell. If fakelore sells better than folklore, then it is fakelore which will be mass produced for tourists and the export market. Folklorismus, the commercialization of folklore, often results in fakelore of this exploitative kind. But folklorismus[54] and fakelore are not really new at all. What is new is the fact that folklorists have finally recognized their existence and have begun to study them seriously.

This brief survey of Ossian, the *Kinder- und Hausmärchen*, and the *Kalevala* is intended to suggest that fakelore did not begin in twentieth-century America. It occurred in the United States only after forces of nationalism came to the fore. It was really only after World War I that the United States began to emerge as a world power, and one could not expect Americans to feel any sense of romantic nostalgia for the past until they had existed as a nation for some years first. Paul Bunyan, it seems to me, is a folk figure of the same epic proportions as an Ossian or a Väinämöinen. He symbolizes America's great size and strength. He is concerned with clearing the land, with making profit from its rich natural resources. An an American self-image, it may be significant that he is not depicted as being very bright. He is no trickster, no clever manipulator. He solves problems through brute strength and a strong will, not through artful diplomacy.

It seems pointless in one sense to argue that the Paul Bunyan figure produced by writers is "ersatz."[55] It is far better to accept the fact that fakelore may be an integral element of culture just as folklore is. Rather than reject fakelore on the a priori grounds that it is impure or bastardized folklore, let us study it as folklorists, using the tools of folkloristics.

NOTES

1. Richard M. Dorson, "Fakelore," *Zeitschrift für Volkskunde* 65 (1969): 60.

2. Richard M. Dorson, *Folklore and Fakelore: Essays toward a Discipline of Folk Studies* (Cambridge, Mass.: Harvard University Press, 1976), p. 5.

3. Ibid., p. 7.

4. Daniel Hoffman, *Paul Bunyan: Last of the Frontier Demigods* (Philadelphia: University of Pennsylvania Press, 1952), p. 74; Richard M.

Dorson, *American Folklore* (Chicago: University of Chicago Press, 1959), pp. 217–18.

5. Edith Fowke, "In Defense of Paul Bunyan," *New York Folklore* 5 (1979): 43–51.

6. Richard M. Dorson, "Folklore and Fakelore," *American Mercury* 70 (1950): 338.

7. Phyllis A. Harrison, "Samuel Johnson's Folkloristics," *Folklore* 94 (1983): 57–65.

8. David Hume, *Essays: Moral, Political and Literary* (London: Longmans, 1898), Vol. 2, pp. 415–24.

9. Neil R. Grobman, "David Hume and the Earliest Scientific Methodology for Collecting Balladry," *Western Folklore* 34 (1975): 29.

10. David Hume, *The Letters of David Hume*, ed. J. Y. T. Greig (Oxford: Clarendon Press, 1932), Vol. 1, p. 399.

11. Neil R. Grobman, "Eighteenth-Century Scottish Philosophers on Oral Tradition," *Journal of the Folklore Institute* 10 (1973): 193; idem, "David Hume and the Earliest Scientific Methodology," p. 29.

12. Derick S. Thomson, *The Gaelic Sources of Macpherson's "Ossian"* (Folcroft, Pa.: Folcroft Press, 1969).

13. Ibid., pp. 29, 55.

14. Ibid., p. 71.

15. Baily Saunders, *The Life and Letters of James Macpherson* (New York: Haskell House, 1968), pp. 9, 140.

16. Ibid., p. 252.

17. Ibid., p. 174.

18. Ibid., pp. 180, 190, 249.

19. John M. Ellis, *One Fairy Story Too Many: The Brothers Grimm and Their Tales* (Chicago: The University of Chicago Press, 1983).

20. Ibid., p. 32. See also Heinz Rölleke, "The 'Utterly Hessian' Fairy Tales by 'Old Marie': The End of a Myth," in Ruth B. Bottigheimer, ed., *Fairy Tales and Society: Illusion, Allusion, and Paradigm* (Philadelphia: University of Pennsylvania Press, 1986), pp. 287–300.

21. Ibid., p. 96.

22. Ibid., p. 100.

23. William A. Wilson, *Folklore and Nationalism in Modern Finland* (Bloomington: Indiana University Press, 1976), p. 40.

24. Jouko Hautala, *Finnish Folklore Research 1828–1918* (Helsinki: Societas Scientarum Fennica, 1968), p. 104; Wilson, *Folklore and Nationalism*, pp. 74–75.

25. Hautala, *Finnish Folklore Research*, p. 120; Wilson, *Folklore and Nationalism*, p. 75; cf. Hans Fromm, "Elias Lönnrot als Schöpfer des finnischen Epos Kalevala," in *Volksepen der uralischen und altaischen Völker*, ed. Wolfgang Veenker, Ural-Altaischen Bibliothek 16 (Wiesbaden: Otto Harrassowitz, 1968), pp. 1–12.

26. Wilson, *Folklore and Nationalism*, p. 75.

27. Ibid., p. 123.

28. Olli Alho, "On Nationalism in a National Science," *Acta Sociologica* 20 (1977): 293–99; Aimo Turunen, "Folk Epic to National Epic: *Kalevala* and *Kalevipoeg*," in *Folklorica: Festschrift for Felix J. Oinas*, ed. Egle Victoria Žygas and Peter Voorheis, Indiana University Uralic and Altaic Series 141 (Bloomington: Research Institute for Inner Asian Studies, 1982), pp. 277–89.

29. Otto A. Webermann, "Kreutzwalds 'Kalevipoeg': Zur Problematik des estnischen Epos," in *Volksepen der uralischen und altaischen Völker, pp. 13–35; Aimo Turunen, "Folk Epic to National Epic."*

30. *Richard M. Dorson, "The American Folk Scene, 1963," Folklore* 74(1963):439; cf. William S. Fox, "Folklore and Fakelore: Some Sociological Considerations," *Journal of the Folklore Institute* 17 (1980): 251.

31. Hoffman, *Paul Bunyan*, p. 97; Edith Fowke, "In Defense of Paul Bunyan," p. 45.

32. Saunders, *The Life and Letters of James Macpherson*, pp. 183–87, 196.

33. Hume, *Letters*, Vol. 2, p. 310.

34. Hume, *Essays*, Vol. 2, p. 416.

35. Grobman, "David Hume and the Earliest Scientific Methodology," p. 18.

36. Hugh Trevor-Roper, "The Invention of Tradition; The Highland Tradition of Scotland," in *The Invention of Tradition*, ed. Eric Hobsbawm and Terence Ranger (Cambridge: Cambridge University Press, 1983), p. 18.

37. Ellis, *One Fairy Story Too Many*, p. 3.

38. Wilson, *Folklore and Nationalism*, p. 5.

39. Ibid., pp. 19–20.

40. Fowke, "In Defense of Paul Bunyan," pp. 44–47.

41. Dorson, *American Folklore*, pp. 216–17.

42. Hobsbawm and Ranger, eds., *The Invention of Tradition*, p. 8.

43. Trevor-Roper, "The Invention of Tradition; The Highland Tradition of Scotland."

44. Cf. Edward Shils, *Tradition* (Chicago: University of Chicago Press, 1981), p. 62.

45. For example, on Finland, see Wilson, *Folklore and Nationalism* and W. R. Mead, "Kalevala and the Rise of Finnish Nationality," *Folklore* 73(1962):217–29; on Greece, see Michael Herzfeld, *Ours Once More: Folklore, Ideology and the Making of Modern Greece* (Austin: The University of Texas Press, 1982); on Russia, see Felix J. Oinas, "The Political Uses and Themes of Folklore in the Soviet Union," *Journal of the Folklore Institute* 12 (1975): 157–75.

46. Cf. Hermann Bausinger, "Volksideologie und Volksforschung: Zur national-sozialistischen Volkskunde," *Zeitschrift für Volkskunde* 61 (1965):1–8; Wolfgang Emmerich, *Zur Kritik der Volkstumsideologie*

(Frankfurt am Main: Suhrkamp, 1971); Christa Kamanetsky, "Folklore as a Political Tool in Nazi Germany," *Journal of American Folklore* 85 (1972): 221–35; idem, "Folktale and Ideology in the Third Reich," *Journal of American Folklore* 90 (1977): 168–78.

47. Wolfgang Mieder, "Proverbs in Nazi Germany: The Promulgation of Anti-Semitism and Stereotypes through Folklore," *Journal of American Folklore* 95 (1982): 458.

48. Richard M. Dorson, "Fakelore," *Zeitschrift für Volkskunde* 65 (1969): 64.

49. Fox, "Folklore and Fakelore," p. 251.

50. Joseph Hanse, "Le centenaire de 'La Légende d'Ulenspiegel,' " *Bulletin de l'Académie Royale de Langue et le Littérature Françaises* 45 (1967): 85–86; Alois Gerlo, "*La Légende d'Ulenspiegel* van Charles De Coster en Vlaanderen," *Revue de l'Université de Bruxelles* 21 (1968–1969): 47.

51. Rudolf Braun, *Socialer und kultureller Wandel in einem ländlichen Industriegebiet im 19. und 20. Jahrhundert* (Erlenbach-Zürich: E. Rentsch, 1965), pp. 327–36.

52. Alsace C. Yen, "Red China's Use of Folklore," *Literature East and West* 8 (1964):72–87; Chung-chiang Yen, "Folklore Research in Communist China," *Asian Folklore Studies* 26 (1967): 1–62.

53. Oinas, "The Political Uses."

54. Cf. Hermann Bausinger, "Folklorismus in Europa: Eine Umfrage," *Zeitschrift für Volkskunde* 65 (1969): 1–8.

55. Dorson, "Fakelore," p. 60.

The Anthropologist and the
Comparative Method in Folklore

Many if not most academic disciplines are comparative in nature and scope. One thinks of comparative law, comparative literature, and comparative religion as typical examples of fields that even contain the very word "comparative," as if to convey just how indispensable the comparative approach is to their nominal identity. More than five hundred periodicals and monograph series include the word in their official titles, which suggests that one form or another of the comparative method informs a goodly number of the conventional natural and social sciences as well as the humanities. It might be a profitable undertaking to make a *comparative* study of all the comparative methods employed in these diverse academic subdivisions, but such a task would require a book-length investigation.

An examination of various comparative methods would almost certainly reveal that many of the same problems are strenuously debated in each of the comparative disciplines. What is the nature of the unit being compared? Is the comparison to be a limited or controlled one or is it to be global in nature? Is there a special form of the comparative method unique to a particular discipline?

Anthropology and folklore are no exceptions and both have utilized a comparative framework, especially in the nineteenth century. Yet the use and refinement of the comparative method have taken very different courses in anthropology and in folklore. Anthropology has tended to turn away from the comparative method, while folklore has steadfastly continued to consider it as its *sine qua non* among competing methodologies.

Anthropology in its beginnings was unmistakably comparative. If one were to consider Herodotus as a precursor of anthropologists, it is clear that he evinced a keen interest in comparing Greek customs with those of neighboring peoples. Singling out one particular time period or one particular individual's work as the starting point of anthropology is difficult if not impossible. One candidate might be the Jesuit priest Joseph-François Lafitau (1670–1740) whose magnum opus *Moeurs des sauvages Ameriquains, comparées aux moeurs des premiers temps* (1724) sought to compare American Indian cultures with those of classical antiquity.[1] But these and the writings of Montesquieu and Voltaire, among others, which drew on early travelers' accounts for their ethnographic data were "illustrative rather than comparative."[2] The identical criticism may apply equally well to late nineteenth- and early twentieth-century compilers such as Frazer. "Examples were cited in support of some thesis deductively arrived at, and in a quite unsystematic way."[3]

If we place the comparative method as practiced by Tylor, Frazer and others at the end of the nineteenth century in intellectual context, we can see that the rationale was not really so unsystematic. The critical underlying premise was that of unilinear evolution, in which it was assumed that *all* peoples had progressed or were progressing from initial savagery through barbarism to the final stage of civilization. Inasmuch as it was (wrongly) understood that all forms of savagery were absolutely identical—and that the ancestors of "civilized" Englishmen and Frenchmen were equivalent to present-day savages and primitives—it made perfect sense to invoke the comparative method. Fragmentary survivals among European peasants could, and indeed it was thought should, be compared to the "original" fuller form of such practices as might still be observed among contemporary savage peoples.

The first chapter of Andrew Lang's 1884 *Custom and Myth*, entitled "The Method of Folklore," spells out the rationale for this form of the comparative method. "There is a form of study, Folklore, which collects and *compares* [my emphasis] the similar but immaterial relics of old races, the surviving superstitions and stories, the ideas which are in our time but not of it."[4] In Lang's terms, "The student of folklore is thus led to examine the usages, myths and ideas of savages, which are still retained in rude enough shape, by the European peasantry."[5] The apparent irrationality of folklore could be explained by understanding such folklore in the light of primitive thought where it was intelligible. "In proverbs and riddles, and nursery tales and superstitions, we detect the relics of a stage of thought, which is dying out in Europe, but which still exists in many parts of the world."[6] This is surely analogous to Lévy-Bruhl's later attempt to define what he called pre-logical or primitive mentality.[7] According to this somewhat racist, ethnocentric theory, primitive people were incapable of thinking in terms of causal logic, a view echoed in the mid-twentieth century by C. G. Jung.

In Jung's essay "The Psychology of the Child Archetype," he maintained that "Primitive mentality differed from the civilized. . . . Functions such as thinking, willing, etc., are not yet differentiated . . . and in the case of thinking, for instance, this shows itself in the circumstance that the primitive does not think consciously, but that thoughts *appear*. The primitive cannot assert that he thinks; it is rather that 'something thinks in him.' "[8]

These and other varieties of the comparative method were formulated by nineteenth-century armchair theorists who had little or no actual contact with so-called primitive peoples. The onset of rigorous fieldwork dealt a death blow to such highly speculative comparative musings. (One of the few exceptions was the pioneering Finnish anthropologist Westermarck who did both extensive fieldwork—in Morocco—and comprehensive library comparative research.[9]) Franz Boas in his 1896 essay "The Limitations of the Comparative Method of Anthropology" argued against the stultifying unilinear evolutionary theory espoused by Tylor, Lang and others.

> It must, therefore, be clearly understood that anthropological research which compares similar cultural phenomena from various parts of the world, in order to discover the uniform history of their development, makes the assumption that the same ethnological phenomenon has everywhere developed in the same manner. Here lies the flaw in the argument of the new method, for no such proof can be given. Even the most cursory review shows that the same phenomena may develop in a multitude of ways.[10]

Since totems, geometrical designs, and the use of masks may each have developed from different sources, they cannot be treated as universals. As Boas so aptly put it, "before extended comparisons are made, the comparability of the material must be proved."[11]

Boas insisted that historical, in-depth studies of individual cultures had to precede comparative studies. In contrasting the "historical method" that he favored against the "comparative method," he felt the inductive, empirical advantages of the former were vastly preferable to the process of "forcing phenomena into the strait-jacket of a theory" involved in the latter. He concluded, "The comparative method, notwithstanding all that has been said and written in its praise, has been remarkably barren of definite results."[12]

Yet Boas, despite his strong reaction to the form of the comparative method advocated by unilinear evolutionists, never did abandon the comparative method in his own research, especially that which pertained to folkloristic data. Although he never adopted the techniques of the Finnish method per se, he was adamantly comparativistic in his treatment of Northwest Coast American Indian myths and tales. His theoretical biases were really quite similar to those of the founders of the Finnish method. He invariably assumed monogenesis and diffusion to explain narrative parallels rather than polygenetic independent invention. In "The Growth of Indian Mythologies: A Study Based upon the Growth of the Mythologies of the North Pacific Coast," presented at a meeting of the American Folklore Society in 1895, Boas articulated his comparative credo:

> If we have a full collection of the tales and myths of all the tribes of a certain region, and then tabulate the number of incidents which all the collections from each tribe have in common with any selected tribe, the number of common incidents will be the larger the more intiate the relation of the two tribes and the nearer they live together. This is what we observe in a tabulation of the material collected on the North Pacific Coast. On the whole, the nearer the people, the greater the number of common elements; the farther apart, the less the number.[13]

Boas was to continue his comparative approach. In perhaps his major work, *Tsimshian Mythology*, published in 1916, Boas after presenting some five hundred pages of Tsimshian myths and tales included an extended section of more than three hundred pages entitled "Comparative Study of Tsimshian Mythology."[14] Similarly, in his 1935 *Kwakiutl Culture as Reflected in Mythology*, Boas concluded with a section entitled "Comparison of Cultural Reflections and Style in Kwakiutl and Tsimshian Mythologies," one of the first studies comparing the images of two peoples on the basis of their respective mythologies.[15]

It should be pointed out that Boas's use of the comparative method was of a strictly limited nature, e.g., confined in some cases to just two tribes or peoples. This notion of a controlled comparison has enjoyed some vogue in anthropological circles. Fred Eggan, for example, indicated "My own preference is for the utilization of the comparative method on a smaller scale and with as much control over the frame of comparison as it is possible to secure."[16] Such a plea for small-scale or limited comparative studies was repeated by others.[17] Herskovits, one of Boas's prize students, suggested that one way to limit the comparative approach was to compare cultures "within a given historic stream."[18] This was no doubt because of Herskovits's special interest in comparing African with Afro-American materials (including folklore) in the New World.

The idea of limited comparative studies, however, did not really address the issue of whether extensive cross-cultural comparisons were methodologically feasible. One of the most serious obstacles in any kind of comparative anthropology concerns the lack of consistency about the "nature of the units between which comparison is being made."[19] The ultimate model for comparative units appears to be from the natural sciences, but the problem is that the units in anthropology such as "bride price" or "patrilineal descent" are not nearly so rigorous as those employed by natural scientists, e.g., atoms and genes.[20] As Herskovits phrased the matter, "We can ask, first of all, what we are comparing."[21]

One of the earliest and most inventive attempts to seek cross-cultural correlations between two or more elements of culture was made by E. B. Tylor. In effect, Tylor combined the evolutionary form of the comparative method with the search for correlations he termed "adhesions." In an important paper "On a Method of

Investigating the Development of Institutions; Applied to Laws of Marriage and Descent," published in 1889, Tylor, using statistics, attempted to demonstrate among other things that the custom of couvade could be correlated with the supposed evolutionary shift from matrilineal to patrilineal societies, and that avoidance behavior could be correlated with postnuptial residence patterns.[22] This innovative paper has been credited by some scholars as the beginning of the comparative method in anthropology.[23] In the discussion which followed immediately upon the presentation of Tylor's paper, Francis Galton, then president of the Anthropological Institute, raised a critical methodological issue. Galton observed, "It was extremely desirable for the sake of those who may wish to study the evidence for Dr. Tylor's conclusions, that full information should be given as to the degree in which the customs of the tribes and races which are compared together are independent. It might be, that some of the tribes had derived them from a common source, so that they were duplicate copies of the same original."[24] The issue, one of source criticism, was: how many independent correlations was Tylor actually citing?[25] What appeared on the surface as a series of cross-cultural correlations might in fact be merely a single instance of a correlation. Galton's remarks have had an enormous inhibiting effect upon the conduct of statistically comparative studies in anthropology and they have even been elevated to the status of being labeled "Galton's problem." It is perhaps one of the few recorded instances where ad hoc discursive remarks following the presentation of a formal paper have had a decisive impact upon the course of scholarship.[26]

As more and more individual ethnographies were written, it became obvious that it was virtually impossible to include every known people or culture in a full-fledged comparative crosscultural investigation. Instead, an alternative strategy was to make use of a random sample of diverse cultures. This program was facilitated by the creation of the Human Relations Area Files in the late 1930s. But HRAF-inspired studies have never become mainstream anthropology.[27] Instead, under the sway and appeal of cultural relativism, social and cultural anthropologists chose to carry out in-depth studies of individual cultures. This shift from comparative literary "armchair" research to field research was one of the most important movements in social anthropology in the twentieth century.[28]

The upshot is that despite a series of essays paying lip service to the comparative method in anthropology by a host of leading anthropologists, notably in the 1950s, the comparative method was essentially abandoned by the majority of anthropologists by the middle of the twentieth century.[29] Whereas Boas had never really ceased to at least cite possible parallels to his mythological texts, many anthropologists who followed him paid little or no heed to the comparative method. Geertz, for instance, writes with insight about a Balinese cockfight, but he makes no reference whatsoever to the abundant scholarship devoted to the cockfight in other cultures.[30] Beidelman analyzes a Kaguru folktale from East Africa as a model of matrilineal dynamics.[31] In a note in a subsequent essay, he remarks, "Since publishing this [earlier study], it has come to my attention that Werner published a somewhat similar tale."[32] The fact that the Kaguru tale he has studied is an example of a standard African tale type, namely, motif K231.1.1, "Mutual agreement to sacrifice family members in famine," was evidently beyond Beidelman's range of knowledge. A simple cursory glance at the *Motif-Index* would have yielded references to a dozen or so additional texts. More than one hundred versions of this tale are in print and the geographical distribution runs from India to New World Afro-American tradition, though the bulk of the reported texts come from sub-Saharan Africa. Beidelman's ignorance of the standard comparative apparatus employed by folklorists is unfortunately not atypical.[33]

It is always an error to analyze a folktale (or any other folkloristic item) as if it were unique to a given cultural context, when it is obviously not so. Beidelman's remarks on the Kaguru version of a standard tale type are not necessarily wrong, but if the same tale were found in a patrilineal society, it would tend to weaken his overall argument that the tale exists as a peculiar response to the pressures of interpersonal relationships caused by Kaguru matrilineality. Anthropologists who blithely assume that a tale they collected from an informant in their limited geographical or cultural area of expertise is totally unique run the risk of making terribly naive and erroneous analyses.

What is the comparative method developed by folklorists about which the anthropologists know so little? It was obvious from the earliest studies of folklore that one could not possibly be a proper folklorist without being comparative. In the first decades of the nineteenth century, the Grimm brothers soon discovered that the tales they collected had close analogues in other countries. Just as historically related languages could be shown to have cognate lexical items and parallel syntactic structures, so folktales and other forms of folklore could be shown to demonstrate genetically/historically common traits.

In the nineteenth century, the reigning intellectual paradigm was historical reconstruction of the past. The dogged attempts to reconstruct the presumed original language from which all subsequent Indo-European languages derived was an inspiration to folklorists.[34] As there might be a hypothetical proto-Indo-European language, so there was thought to be a hypothetical proto- or *Ur-form* for any particular myth found among Indo-European peoples. The methodology employed was distinctly comparative in nature. One compared as many versions of the myth (or whatever genre) as possible from as many different cultures as possible. According to what was later to be labeled in anthropology as the age-area hypothesis, it was assumed that the more widespread a myth (or a trait contained in a myth) was, the older it was. Thus *geographical* distribution was understood to be an important criterion of age (although this remains a largely unproved assumption rather than an empirically documented fact[35]). In addition, the historic record often proved useful. Any literary or early written versions of a myth could provide a tentative *terminus ante quem*. So the existence of actual dated texts permitted some *historical* basis for the presumed ancestral form. The combination of the historical and geographical criteria for determining the hypothetical original form or home of a given myth led eventually to the designation of the method as "historic-geographic."

The centrality of the so-called Finnish method in folkloristics is revealed by a simple review of the titles of three publications by Kaarle Krohn (1863–1933), who is generally credited with refining the standard version of the comparative method adopted by most folklorists. In 1889, he presented a paper at the Congrès International des Traditions Populaires in Paris. In the proceedings of the congress Krohn's paper is entitled "La methode de M. Jules Krohn."[36] Krohn begins by speaking of the major work of his father Julius (1835–1888), which had consisted of a comparative study of Kalevala verses. Kaarle Krohn had applied this same method to folktales for his doctoral dissertation, which he had defended at the University of Helsinki in 1887, two years before the Paris conference. In the foreword to his published dissertation (1888), Krohn had specifically remarked "Finally, I wish to point out that my research method is the same geographic-historical one that my father, Professor Julius Krohn, used in his Kalevalian studies and which in all folklore research, on the whole, represents the only right way to go."[37]

In a lecture given on 31 January 1909, Krohn had re-christened the name of the method. The paper, published in 1910, was entitled "Über die finnische folkloristische Methode."[38] So the original method of his father had become the "Finnish" method. But in 1907, Krohn had already been instrumental in forming the Folklore Fellows (with Olrik of Denmark, Bolte of Germany, von Sydow of Sweden) and he began to become more international in outlook. Near the end of his distinguished career, Kaarle Krohn published a basic primer delineating the principles involved in the comparative method. This work, based upon invited lectures in 1924 at the Norwegian Instituttet for Sammenlignende Kulturforskning, was published in 1926 as *Die folkloristische Arbeitsmethode, begründet von Julius Krohn und weitergeführt von nordischen Forschern.*[39] Note that the title was not "*Eine* folkloristische Arbeitsmethode," but rather "*Die* folkloristische Arbeitsmethode." So the evolution was complete. From the method of his father as presented in 1889 to the Finnish method of the 1909 period, we now had *the* folkloristic method! And in some sense, the comparative method as developed by Krohn and his students, notably Aarne, has remained the centerpiece of folkloristics. Accordingly, Honko in his (1979–1980) survey of "Methods in Folk-Narrative Research: Their Status and Future" begins with a review of the comparative method.[40]

Although Honko claims that "The method *originated in Finland* during the latter half of the nineteenth century through the works of Julius and Kaarle Krohn, father and son . . . and has been called the 'historical-geographical' or 'Finnish' method ever since," this may be an illustration of excessive nationalistic zeal.[41] The comparative method per se did not originate in Finland. It was part of a greater intellectual movement that belonged to a variety of disciplines. The Grimms, for example, were as much interested in comparative philology as in comparative mythology. Perhaps the popularity of comparative anatomy and the research of Cuvier and others inspired the comparativism of Jacob Grimm.[42] Max Müller, for example, published his extensive essay on comparative mythology in 1856. Archer Taylor in "Precursors of the Finnish Method of Folk-Lore Study" claimed that the principles involved in the Finnish method were used before the Krohns, calling attention in particular to the comparative approach employed by the Danish scholar Svend Grundtvig in his remarkable compilation of Danish ballads that began to appear in 1853.[43] Taylor concludes, "The Finnish method is therefore a procedure which was already being employed elsewhere and which, if it had not been formulated by Finnish scholars, would have found formulation sooner or later in France and Germany. Yet the codification was itself so significant a step forward that we shall not begrudge the Finns the method's name."[44] So the comparative method as practiced by the Krohns may well owe something to the prior work of Grundtvig just as Aarne's original formulation of the tale-type index may have been partially inspired by Astrid Lunding's *The System of Tales in the Folktale Collection of Copenhagen*, again a reflection of Grundtvig's efforts. Lunding's tabulation was, after all, published as *FFC* No. 2. Aarne's *Verzeichnis der Märchentypen* was *FFC* No. 3, which may or may not be an index of priority.

Perhaps the same strong feelings of nationalism in Finland that led to the early scholarly interest in the nation's folklore was partly responsible for Finnish scholars insisting that their refinement of the standard comparative method (employed, for example, in stemma manuscript research) be called the "Finnish" method. In this context, can it be only coincidence that scholars from Russia and Sweden were the ones who felt compelled to critique the Finnish method? Or was it an understandable reaction to the nationalism of the Finns? Von Sydow was especially devastating: "But as the Finnish school have for the most part been content to study extracts, the life of the tradition has escaped them; and instead they have built on a number of postulates constructed in the air without connection with reality; and so these laboriously produced monographs must be considered as mistaken in their chief results."[45] In the same vein, he continues "We must build our research on the life and laws of the tradition, not on dry and lifeless extracts. The flesh which research puts on such dry lifeless bones is, and remains, dead, without connection with a living reality, and therefore without value."[46]

The champions of the Finnish method in the United States were Archer Taylor and Stith Thompson. While Taylor applied the method to essentially European folkloristic data, Thompson was a bit more creative. He encouraged his students to utilize the method in the study of American Indian folktales. In his 1953 investigation of the "Star Husband" tale (derived from a 1931 M.A. thesis by his student, Edith Gore Campbell),[47] Thompson specifically notes the advantages of considering a purely oral tale. In studies of European tales, the influence of literary, written versions upon oral tales is inevitably a problem. This difficulty was totally obviated by using American Indian versions of a tale type collected from oral tradition. So while American anthropologists failed to take any notice of the Finnish method in their occasional considerations of American Indian tales, Thompson and his students (for example, van Winkle in 1959[48]) applied this European methodology to American Indian data. Incidentally, I do not believe that many (if any) of these Finnish method investigations of American Indian tales have been discussed by European folklorists, perhaps because they exist only as unpublished theses or dissertations.

In a polite way Thompson drew attention to the fact that anthropologists interested in folklore refused to use the established techniques of the Finnish method. "Star Husband," the tale studied by Thompson, was examined comparatively by Gladys Reichard, a prominent student of Boas, who possessed great expertise in

American Indian folklore. Thompson observes that Reichard "proceeded by a somewhat different method from that here employed."[49] In a 1921 essay, "Literary Types and Dissemination of Myths," Reichard examined Star Husband, Lodge-Boy and Thrown-Away, and Earthdiver. On the basis of some 51 versions of Star Husband, she divided the tale into 8 traits (A-H) although she did not use the term "trait." She preferred the term "episode." The first trait, (A) Wish for husband, is subdivided into (1) Each girl for star, and (2) One girl for star. Twenty-nine versions of "Star Husband" are broken down into constituent episodes, e.g., Koasati is A1B1E2F2. The notational format is strikingly similar to the Finnish method. Thompson in 1953 used 86 versions for his corpus and had 14 traits (A-N). Reichard was able to suggest a normal form of the tale: "We may say that the 'Star-Husband' story consists of the following main elements: (1) the wish for a husband, (2) ascent to sky, (3) taboo and its infringement, (4) birth of son, (5) descent to earth, (6) death of mother."[50] Reichard also distinguished three different classes of the tale, which she labels Type I, Type II and Type III. We would probably call them subtypes in Finnish method parlance. Thompson identifies six types (as opposed to Reichard's three) but essentially Thompson's Type I, The Basic Tale (Archetype) corresponds to Reichard's Type I, Star-Husband Complex. Moreover, his Type II, The Porcupine Redaction, is close to Reichard's Type II, Star-Husband Complex Plus Adventures of Star-Boy, the summary of which begins: "Girl wishes for celestial husband, is lured to sky by porcupine. . . ."[51]

The point here is not to compare two different comparative studies of the same tale, but rather to suggest that Reichard more or less reinvented the Finnish method to carry out her 1921 comparative study. She even included a map that plotted out the three Star-Husband types to give a rough idea of their respective distribution patterns on the North American continent. No explicit evidence whatsoever indicates that she was familiar with the Finnish method. This study is probably as near as any anthropologist has gotten to employing anything resembling the Finnish method. It demonstrates that (1) anthropologists interested in comparative studies could have profited from a knowledge of the refinements introduced by the Finns and others and (2) that they operated then—and now—in total ignorance of the standard methods used by comparative folklorists.

For the record, we must confess that it may be a bit unfair to compare Thompson's 1953 essay with Reichard's study of 1921. It is by no means clear how much Thompson himself knew in 1921 about the historic-geographic method. He certainly did not know about Aarne's tale-type index in 1914 when he completed his doctoral dissertation at Harvard, a dissertation which was an inventory of European tale types found in American Indian oral tradition. Nor is there any reference whatsoever to the type index in the published version of his dissertation *European Tales among the North American Indians* in 1919, nearly ten years after the publication of Aarne's pioneering work. The *Index* would have been a great convenience to Thompson. As it was, he had to indulge in a somewhat clumsy technique of recounting a rather full synopsis of each European tale before identifying a version from American Indian oral tradition. It would have been easier simply to have referred to the relevant European tale by Aarne number. As it happens, Thompson later confirmed his early ignorance of the tale-type index in his unpublished autobiography "Folklorist's Progress." Late in the summer of 1920, en route to a teaching stint at the University of Maine, Thompson stopped for two weeks in Cambridge, in part to visit the Widener Library at Harvard:

> Among the new books which I found was one that was to be of primary importance in my future. This was Antti Aarne's *Verzeichnis der Märchentypen*, a basic classification of the tales in the European and Asiatic tradition. How much would I have not given to have this when I was working on my own thesis! It had appeared in 1910 but apparently had not yet come to the attention of American scholars. It was so important for me that I managed to borrow it for a while and later made a longhand abstract of the whole thing.[52]

Actually, it had been noticed by American scholars. T. F. Crane of Cornell University, the first great American student of international folktales, knew of the work of Krohn and Aarne. He reviewed the first 21 *FFC*s in 1916.[53]

The folkloristic conception of type turns out to be absolutely critical with respect to the comparative method. The word "compare" literally refers to bringing together "equal" or "similar" elements. The idea is that one should compare only "comparable" items. One sought or assumed similarities, not differences. The word "contrast" implies differences, and that is why to this day, one may ask a student to "compare and contrast" two entities, that is, find both similarities and differences. But if the comparative method was designed to study "similar" items, the question invariably arose as to "how similar is similar?" Were the folkloristic items being compared similar in a vague sense of being roughly analogous—in either structure or content? Or were the items assumed to be cognate, that is, historically and genetically related?

Generally speaking, the concept of type in anthropology did *not* necessarily assume cognation. Thus an anthropologist might speak of a type of social organization or family structure. One could accordingly compare examples of matrilineal or patrilineal social organization, but one could do so without assuming that the peoples possessing such organizational "types" were historically related. One here had comparison without cognation.[54]

In contrast, folklorists for the most part understand something different by the concept of type. Perhaps the most penetrating definition of tale type was written by the brilliant Hungarian folklorist Hans Honti in 1939. He suggested that there were three possible ways of looking at the tale type as a unit. First the tale type binds together a number of motifs. Second, the tale type stands as an individual entity in contrast with other tale types. Third, the tale type is manifested in multiple appearances called variants.[55] So a tale type consists of manifestations or versions of one particular, identifiable plot line. Cinderella, Aarne-Thompson tale type 510A, is a specific story different from Little Red Riding Hood, Aarne-Thompson tale type 333. Whereas anthropologists sloppily use "Cinderella" to refer loosely to American Indian tales in which an unpromising heroine gains a husband, folklorists would not use "Cinderella" for anything except versions of tale type 510A.

For folklorists, the comparative method normally assumes that cognate materials are being investigated. Kaarle Krohn makes this perfectly clear when he begins his discussion of "identity" by stating "In reconstructing a basic form, it must further be assumed that the variants being compared all go back to one parent form."[56]

To be sure, folklorist Heda Jason claims "No necessary genetic connection exists between texts told in the field" in her discussion of the tale type concept,[57] but this is not a majority view among professional folklorists. The Finnish method's assumption of cognation is intimately related to the bias in favor of monogenesis. Krohn is once again unambiguous on this matter: "Polygenesis in the most extreme sense, that every variant was composed separately at innumerable sites, is unthinkable."[58] On the contrary, "it must also be assumed of these that each individual form arose at one particular location."[59]

The distinction between genetic and non-genetic types, or if one prefers, cognate and non-cognate types, is absolutely critical in distinguishing the comparative method as employed by anthropologists on the one hand and by folklorists on the other. The Finnish method is designed to study cognate parallels, that is, the variations of a particular tale or ballad or proverb type. Anthropologists are more interested in general, not specific, typological comparisons, which may be one reason why they have eschewed the Finnish method. By the same token, on those occasions where anthropologists have sought to investigate cognate phenomena, they might well have profited from a knowledge of the Finnish method.

The most important criticism of both anthropologists *and* folklorists is that they have failed equally to employ a broader, more comprehensive form of the comparative method. Consequently, neither anthropologists nor folklorists have succeeded in discovering general laws or principles of culture. The anthropologists have never recovered from the abandonment of the comparative method in the nineteenth century. Their abiding commitment to the principle of cultural relativism—which ultimately insists that each separate and distinct culture is a noncomparable monad—had led to a bewildering number of excellent ethnographic monographs, but it has not facilitated the formulation of a set of testable cross-cultural, that is, comparative hypotheses. The quest for general laws or large-scale theoretical postulates has bogged down with the weight of dozens upon dozens of ethnographies.

Folklorists in contrast have never recovered from their obsessive insistence upon the comparative method. The lore is considered independent of the folk who produce and transmit it. Superorganic laws of form and transmission are postulated (cf. Olrik and Aarne) but with little or no reference to living human beings (or psychology).[60] The inordinate amount of time and effort required to complete even one full-fledged historic-geographic study of a tale type precludes the possibility of generalizing about folktales. Supposedly, we must await the results of comparative studies of all folktales before we can safely speculate about the meaning of the folktale as a genre. Stith Thompson remarks, "When the folklorist has done his best to discover all the facts about the life history of the tale, there may be room for the psychologist, and the sociologist and the anthropologist."[61] But it is frankly not possible for the folklorist to discover *all* the facts about a given folktale, for the written record goes back only so far and oral tales clearly antedate written languages. So in Thompson's terms, there will never be a time when psychologists, sociologists, and anthropologists would be welcome to investigate folktales.

The sad truth is that the accumulated impact of all the historic-geographic studies ever undertaken is minimal. No one really believes that one can discover "Kaarle Krohn's dream of the well-balanced, poetically perfect wording of the *Urform*."[62] The Finnish method studies do bring together impressive masses of cognate versions of an item of folklore and it is often possible to discern patterns of distribution along geographical and cultural lines. But to what end? One cannot deny that "There are no far-reaching results from historic-geographic studies, results of theoretical interest."[63] Just as the sum total of all the anthropologists' ethnographies don't add up to anything theoretical, so the sum total of all the folklorists' comparative studies don't add up to anything theoretical.

Most Finnish method monographs are nothing more than glorified distribution studies. Practitioners of the cartographic method still quite popular among European folklorists laboriously and painstakingly plot dots on maps signaling data garnered from questionnaires. One cannot very well blame anthropologists for ignoring the method. What then, if anything, is there to be done with respect to the comparative method in anthropology and folklore?

I believe one key is the concept of *oicotype*.[64] In order to study the relevance of folklore to a culture, or to an individual in that culture, the comparative method is essential. One cannot know a priori what is or is not unique to a culture without seeking possible cognate phenomena in adjacent or historically related cultures. Anyone who wishes to study a Balinese cockfight or a Kaguru folktale in a culturally-relative context should make some attempt to consider cognates of these cultural phenomena elsewhere.

Anthropologists at least show some interest in studying the meaning of folklore! Folklorists employing the comparative method carefully assemble and classify dozens upon dozens of versions of an item of folklore, but they inevitably stop short of studying the meaning of the item—either in general or in a particular cultural context. A comparative study of a folktale, or other form of folklore, may very well yield a definite oicotype, that is, a particular version common to only one particular cultural context. Such data is ideal for the study of how folklore is modified to fit local ideological or world view tendencies. The concept of subtype is not the same as the concept of oicotype. A subtype refers simply to a cluster of traits that may be found in a number of different cultures. It may be difficult to correlate a subtype with one specific culture. In essence, the opportunity of isolating oicotypes from comparative studies has been lost or ignored.

If the comparative method were used to identify oicotypes—and this would be an empirical and hence replicable process—the resultant oicotypes might provide important clues to key characteristics of the culture in question. Not only would it be possible to discern patterns of regional or national character, but the way in which folklore is modified to fit local needs would then be much better understood.

The search for oicotypes depends upon the Finnish method, that is, with the comparison of cognate materials. However, the comparative aspects of folklore research need not be confined to what has been commonly called "the" Finnish or comparative method. That is only one type of comparative method. Just as there are many different possible forms of comparison in anthropology—"between single culture traits, between institutions, between subcultures, between areas, nations, and civilizations"[65]—so there are many possible comparative studies in folklore. Some of the most important findings in folklore have come from a form of the comparative method, but not the Finnish method. For example, Frazer's principles of sympathetic magic, homeopathic and contagious, represent an extrapolation from an assemblage of data. The same principles apparently underlie quite diverse practices.[66] Van Gennep's discovery of a common tripartite pattern in birth, wedding, and funeral rituals depended upon a form of the comparative method.[67] Propp's *Morphology*, which aimed at delineating a common schema for Russian fairy tales (Aarne-Thompson tale types 300–749), came about through a comparison of the constituent elements in 100 consecutive tales in the Afanasiev collection. Structural and comparative studies are not mutually exclusive.

Re-eliciting a text from a single informant could be construed as a form of the comparative method. Even the Freudian model, which postulates a possible correlation between early infant conditioning in a given culture and the folkloristic projections to be found in that culture, involves a comparativist approach, for it entails *comparing* the specifics of such conditioning, e.g., toilet training, and recurrent or dominant themes or tendencies in the folklore.[68]

What we may conclude is that while the Finnish method is the most refined and sophisticated technique yet devised for investigating the distribution patterns of folklore cognates, it should not be identified as "the" comparative method. It is, or should be thought of as, *a* comparative method.[69] And it is a form of the comparative method that could be of great assistance to the anthropologist anxious to isolate peculiarities or unique characteristics of people. It is a method that could facilitate the delineation of truly culturally-relativistic details. Finally, if either anthropology or folklore is to get beyond the data-gathering or data-amassing stage, bolder and more imaginative forms of the comparative method are crucial. Fieldwork and Finnish method studies should not be ends in themselves. They should be the means by which social sciences of anthropology and of folklore are established with definite, testable hypotheses leading eventually to reliable general principles.

NOTES

1. For appreciations of the comparative research of Lafitau, see Arnold van Gennep, "Contributions à l'histoire de la méthode ethnographique," *Revue de l'Histoire des Religions* 67 (1913): 320–38; and P. Saint-yves, "Les Origines de la méthode comparative et la naissance du folklore. Des superstitions aux survivances," *Revue de l'Histoire des Religions* 105 (1932): 44–70. As E. B. Tylor observed, Lafitau was perhaps the first to remark the occurrence of the motif of the earth resting on a turtle's back (Motif A844.1) in India and native North America. See Edward B. Tylor, *Early History of Mankind* (Chicago: University of Chicago Press, 1964), p. 202.

In light of the thesis to be advanced in this paper, it is relevant that the twentieth-century anthropologists who have commented on this motif seem to be ignorant of its existence in Asia. They speak only of its function among the Iroquois or Delaware. See William N. Fenton, "This Island, The World on The Turtle's Back," *Journal of American Folklore* 75 (1962): 283–300; and Jay Miller, "Why the World Is on the Back of a Turtle," *Man*, N.S. 9 (1974): 306–308.

2. E. E. Evans-Pritchard, *The Comparative Method in Social Anthropology*, L. T. Hobhouse Memorial Trust Lecture No. 33 (London: The Athlone Press, 1963), p. 4.

3. Ibid.

4. Andrew Lang, *Custom and Myth* (London: Longmans, Green, and Co., 1884), p. 11.

5. Ibid.

6. Lang, pp. 12–13.

7. See, for example, Lucien Lévy-Bruhl, *Primitive Mentality* (Boston: Beacon Press, 1966); *The Notebooks on Primitive Mentality* (New York: Harper & Row, 1975). For a useful discussion of the concept, see Jean Cazaneuve, *Lucien Lévy-Bruhl* (New York: Harper & Row, 1972), pp. 3–23.

8. C. G. Jung, "The Psychology of the Child Archetype," in C. G. Jung and C. Kerenyi, *Essays on a Science of Mythology* (New York: Harper & Row, 1963), p. 72.

9. Edmund Leach in his essay "The Comparative Method in Anthropology" singles out Edward Westermarck as an exception to the rule that armchair comparativists never left the library for the field. See Leach, "Anthropology: Comparative Method," in David L. Sills, ed., *International Encyclopedia of the Social Sciences*, Vol. 1 (New York: The Macmillan Company & The Free Press, 1968), p. 342. For more about this unusual early anthropologist, see Ragnar Numelin, *Fältforskare och kammarlarde: Drag ur socialantropologiens idéhistoria* (Stockholm: Hugo Gebers Förlag, 1947), pp. 80–91, and Timothy Stroup, *Edward Westermarck: Essays on His Life and Works, Acta Philosophica Fennica* 34 (1982).

10. "The Limitations of the Comparative Method of Anthropology," *Science*, N.S. 4 (1896): 901–908, reprinted in *Race, Language and Culture* (New York: Macmillan, 1940), pp. 270–80. For the quotation, see p. 273.

11. Boas, p. 275.

12. Ibid., p. 280.

13. "The Growth of Indian Mythologies," *Journal of American Folklore* 9 (1896): 1–11, reprinted in *Race, Language and Culture*, pp. 425–36. For the quotation, see p. 427. The principle enunciated is strikingly similar to the basic premise underlying what is called glottochronology or lexicostatistics, whereby linguistic parallels are quantified to reveal degrees of relationship between peoples. See Sarah C. Gudschinsky, "The ABC's of Lexicostatistics (Glottochronology)," in Dell Hymes, ed., *Language in Culture and Society* (New York: Harper & Row, 1964), pp. 612–23.

14. *Tsimshian Mythology*, Thirty-First Annual Report of the Bureau of American Ethnology (Washington: Government Printing Office, 1916), pp. 565–881.

15. *Kwakiutl Culture as Reflected in Mythology*, Memoirs of the American Folklore Society 28 (New York: G. E. Stechert, 1935), pp. 171–90.

16. Fred Eggan, "Social Anthropology and the Method of Controlled Comparison," *American Anthropologist* 56 (1954): 747.

17. Evans-Pritchard, op. cit., pp. 20, 22.

18. Melville J. Herskovits, "On Some Modes of Ethnographic Comparison." *Bijdragen Tot de Taal-, Land- en Volkenkunde* 112 (1956): 141.

19. I. Schapera, "Some Comments on Comparative Method in Social Anthropology," *American Anthropologist* 55 (1953): 353. For representative discussions of the critical nature of unit definition for comparative studies, see Terrence A. Tatje, "Problems of Concept Definition for Comparative Studies,' in Raoul Naroll and Ronald Cohen, eds., *A Handbook of Method in Cultural Anthropology* (New York: Columbia University Press, 1970), pp. 689–96, or the section devoted to "units of comparison," in Gopala Śarana, *The Methodology of Anthropological Comparisons: An Analysis of Comparative Methods in Social and Cultural Anthropology*. Viking Fund Publications in Anthropology No. 53. (Tucson: University of Arizona Press, 1975), pp. 18–33. See also Rolf Wirsing, "Probleme des interkulturellen Vergleichs in der Ethnologie," *Sociologus* 25 (1975): 97–126.

20. Leach, op. cit., p. 341.

21. Herskovits, op. cit., p. 135.

22. *Journal of the Royal Anthropological Institute of Great Britain and Ireland* 18 (1889): 245–72.

23. E. A. Hammel, "The Comparative Method in Anthropological Perspective," *Comparative Studies in Society and History* 22 (1980): 146.

24. For Galton's comments, see "Discussion," *Journal of the Royal Anthropological Institute of Great Britain and Ireland* 18 (1889): 270.

25. Raoul Naroll, "Galton's Problem," in Naroll and Cohen, *A Handbook of Method*, p. 974.

26. For a sample of the debate inspired by Galton's remarks, see Raoul Naroll, "Some Thoughts on Comparative Method in Cultural Anthropology," in Hubert M. Blalock, Jr., and Ann B. Blalock, eds., *Methodology in Social Research* (New York: McGraw-Hill, 1968), pp. 258–62; Naroll, "Galton's Problem: The Logic of Cross-Cultural Analysis," *Social Research* 32 (1966): 428–51; E. Rosenthal, "Galton's Problem Revisited," *Cornell Journal of Social Relations* 7 (1972): 17–27; and Thomas Schweizer, *Methodenprobleme des interkulturellen Vergleichs*, Kölner Ethnologische Mitteilungen 6 (Köln: Böhlau Verlag, 1978), pp. 132–54.

27. Only a very few professional anthropologists make any extended use of the Human Relations Area Files. One of the more successful and influential research efforts of this type is John N. M. Whiting and Irving L. Child, *Child Training and Personality* (New Haven: Yale University Press, 1953).

28. Evans-Pritchard, op. cit., p. 23. For an account of the sharp division between advocates and detractors of the comparative method in anthropology, see Andre J. F. Köbben, "Comparativists and Non-Comparativists in Anthropology," in Naroll and Cohen, *A Handbook of Method*, pp. 581–96.

29. For this view, see Erwin H. Ackerknecht, "On the Comparative Method in Anthropology," in Robert F. Spencer, ed., *Method and Perspective in Anthropology: Papers in Honor of Wilson D. Wallis* (Minneapolis: University of Minnesota Press, 1954), pp. 117–25. For a sample of the various efforts to reconsider the comparative method in the 1950s, see A. R. Radcliffe-Brown, "The Comparative Method in Social Anthropology," *Journal of the Royal Anthropological Institute* 81 (1951): 15–22; I. Schapera, "Some Comments on Comparative Method in Social Anthropology," *American Anthropologist* 55 (1953): 353–62, plus Milton B. Singer's "Summary of Comments and Discussion," *American Anthropologist* 55 (1953): 362–66; Fred Eggan, "Social Anthropology and the Method of Controlled Comparison," *American Anthropologist* 56 (1954): 743–63; Oscar Lewis, "Comparisons in Cultural Anthropology," in William L. Thomas, Jr., ed., *Yearbook of Anthropology* (1955): 259–92; and Melville J. Herskovits, "On Some Modes of Ethnographic Comparison," *Bijdragen Tot de Taal-, Land- en Volkenkunde* 112 (1956): 129–48. See also the extended discussion of "The Comparative Method" under the rubric of Experimental Anthropology in S. F. Nadel, *The Foundations of Social Anthropology* (London: Cohen & West, 1951), pp. 222–55.

30. The essay in question first appeared in the Winter, 1972 issue of *Daedalus*. See Clifford Geertz, "Deep Play: Notes on the Balinese Cockfight," *Daedalus: Journal of the American Academy of Arts and Sciences* 101 (Winter, 1972): 1–37. Geertz in one footnote (30) does refer briefly to British cockfights and to several books on the subject, but there is no

reference to the vast ethnographic literature on cockfighting. For a partial entrée into the scholarship, see Gerald E. Parsons, "Cockfighting: A Potential Field of Research," *New York Folklore Quarterly* 25 (1969): 265–88. For a representative account of the tradition in the United States published since Geertz's essay, see Steven Del Sesto, "Roles, Rules, and Organization: A Descriptive Account of Cockfighting in Rural Louisiana," *Southern Folklore Quarterly* 39 (1975): 1–14. For data from Mexico, see Maria Justina Sarabia Viejo, *El juego de gallos en Nueva España* (Sevilla: Escuela de Estudios Hispano-Americanos de Sevilla, 1972).

31. T. O. Beidelman, "Hyena and Rabbit: A Kaguru Representation of Matrilineal Relations," *Africa* 33 (1961): 61-74.

32. "Further Adventures of Hyena and Rabbit: The Folktale as a Sociological Model," *Africa* 33 (1963): 54, n. 2.

33. Geneviève Calame-Griaule and Pierre-Francis Lacroix examine the same tale studied by Beidelman in their essay "La 'Mère Vendue': Essai d'analyse d'un theme de conte Africain," in Jean Pouillon and Pierre Maranda, *Echanges et Communications*, II (The Hague: Mouton, 1970), pp. 1356–80. Although they cite ten different texts of the tale, there is no reference to the *Motif-Index* or to the versions listed there. For the majority of anthropologists, it is as if the *Motif-Index* or the tale type index had never been compiled.

34. Many of those who have written on the comparative method have recognized the method's debt to such pioneers of comparative grammar as Franz Bopp (1791–1867). See, for example, Raffaele Pettazzoni, "Il metodo comparativo," *Numen* 6 (1959): 2. There can be no question but that the techniques employed in reconstructing proto-Indo-European were an important model for nineteenth-century comparative folklorists. See A. Meillet, *La Methode comparative en linguistique historique* (Oslo: H. Aschehoug & Co., 1925). It is of more than passing interest that this work whose first chapter (pp. 1–11) constituted a definition of the comparative method was published under the auspices of the Instituttet for Sammenlignende Kulturforskning in Oslo, the same institution which published Kaarle Krohn's primer on the comparative method in folklore the following year. For another account of the linguistic methodology involved, see Paul Thieme, "The Comparative Method for Reconstruction in Linguistics," in Hymes, ed., *Language in Culture and Society*, pp. 585–98.

35. For some of the heated discussion of this alleged principle, see Wilson D. Wallis, "Diffusion as a Criterion of Age," *American Anthropologist* 27 (1925): 91–99; Herbert Jennings Rose, *Concerning Parallels*, The Frazer Lecture 1934 (Oxford: Clarendon Press, 1934), p. 15; Margaret T. Hodgen, "Geographical Diffusion as a Criterion of Age," *American Anthropologist* 44 (1942): 345–68; Wilson D. Wallis, "Inference of Relative Age of Culture Traits from Magnitude of Distribution," *Southwestern Journal of Anthropology* 1 (1945): 142–59; and the entry "Age-and-Area

Theory," in Åke Hultkrantz, *General Ethnological Concepts* (Copenhagen: Rosenkilde and Bagger, 1960), pp. 24–25.

36. Kaarle Krohn, "La méthode de M. Jules Krohn," in *Congrès international des traditions populaires*. Premiere session. (Paris: Société d'éditions scientifiques, 1891), pp. 64–68.

37. Jouko Hautala, "Kaarle Krohn as a Folklorist," *Studia Fennica* 11 (1964): 3–72. For the quotation, see p. 10.

38. Krohn, "Über die finnische folkloristische Methode," *Finnischugrische Forschungen* 10 (1910): 33–43.

39. Oslo: Instituttet for Sammenlignende Kulturforskning, 1926. This work was reprinted in English translation as *Folklore Methodology* (Austin: University of Texas Press, 1971). For later accounts of the method, see Walter Anderson, "Geographische-historische Methode," in Lutz Mackensen, ed., *Handwörterbuch des deutschen Märchens*, Vol. 2 (Berlin and Leipzig: Walter de Gruyter, 1934–1940), pp. 508–22; Bertalan Korompay, *Zur finnischen Methode: Gedanken eines Zeitgenossen* (Helsinki, 1978); and Christine Goldberg, "The Historic-Geographic Method: Past and Future," *Journal of Folklore Research* 21 (1984): 1–18.

40. Lauri Honko, "Methods in Folk-Narrative Research: Their Status and Future," *Ethnologia Europaea* 11 (1979–1980): 6–27.

41. Honko, op. cit., p. 7. The emphasis has been added.

42. Ackerknecht, op. cit., p. 119. See also the valuable survey by Helge Gerndt, "Die Anwendung der vergleichenden Methode in der Europäischen Ethnologie," *Ethnologia Europaea* 10 (1977–1978): 2–32. (The reference to Cuvier is on p. 5).

43. Archer Taylor, "Precursors of the Finnish Method of Folk-Lore Study," *Modern Philology* 25 (1928): 481–91.

44. Ibid., p. 489.

45. C. W. von Sydow, "Geography and Folk-Tale Oicotypes," in *Selected Papers on Folklore* (Copenhagen: Rosenkilde and Bagger, 1948), pp. 45–46.

46. Ibid., p. 59. For more of von Sydow's criticisms of the Finnish method, see his "Finsk metod och modern sagoforskning," *Rig* 26 (1943): 1–23. For a useful summary of the Russian objections to the Finnish method, see Heda Jason, "The Russian Criticism of the 'Finnish School' in Folktale Scholarship," *Norveg* 14 (1970): 285–94.

47. For Thompson's study, see "The Star Husband Tale," *Studia Septentrionalia* 4 (1953): 93–163, reprinted in Alan Dundes, ed., *The Study of Folklore* (Englewood Cliffs, N.J.: Prentice-Hall, 1965), pp. 414–74. For the earlier thesis, see Edith Gore Campbell, " 'The Star Husband Tale': A Comparative Study by the Historic-Geographic Method," (unpublished M.A. thesis in English, Indiana University, 1931, 131 pp.) In a footnote, Thompson acknowledges that the thesis "served as a starting point" for his investigation.

48. Elva Young van Winkle, "The Eye-Juggler: A Tale Type Study"

(unpublished M.A. thesis in folklore, Indiana University, 1959, 156 pp.)
49. Thompson, p. 419, n. 3.
50. Gladys A. Reichard, "Literary Types and Dissemination of Myths," *Journal of American Folklore* 34 (1921): 281.
51. Ibid., pp. 283–84.
52. Stith Thompson, "Folklorist's Progress," (unpublished autobiography, 1956), p. 81.
53. See T. F. Crane, "Review of FF Communications, Nos. 1–21," *Romanic Review* 7 (1916): 110–25. Professor Crane's enormous erudition and remarkable familiarity with international folklore scholarship have never been properly acknowledged in most surveys of American folkloristics.
54. See, for example, J. A. Ford, "On the Concept of Types: The Type Concept Revisited," *American Anthropologist* 56 (1954): 42–57. (This includes a discussion of "Types of Types" by Julian H. Steward, pp. 54–57.)
55. Hans Honti, "Märchenmorphologie und Märchentypologie," *Folk-Liv* 3 (1939): 307–18. For other considerations of the tale type, see Heda Jason "Structural Analysis and the Concept of the 'Tale-type'," *Arv*, 28 (1972): 36–54, and Robert A. Georges "The Universality of the Tale-Type as Concept and Construct," *Western Folklore* 42 (1983): 21–28. See also Dan Ben-Amos, "The Concept of Motif in Folklore," in Venetia J. Newall, ed., *Folklore Studies in the Twentieth Century* (Woodbridge, Suffolk: Brewer, 1980), pp. 17–36; and Joseph Courtés, "Motif et type dans la tradition folklorique: Problèmes de typologie," *Littérature* 45 (February, 1982): 114–27.
56. Krohn, *Folklore Methodology*, p. 126.
57. Jason, "Structural Analysis," p. 53.
58. Krohn, *Folklore Methodology*, p. 136.
59. Ibid, p. 139.
60. For classic illustrations of the superorganic influence upon folkloristics, see Axel Olrik, "Epic Laws of Folk Narrative," in Dundes, *The Study of Folklore*, pp. 129–41, or Antti Aarne's *Leitfaden der vergleichenden Märchenforschung*, FFC 13 (Hamina, 1913) with its attempt to codify the changes that occur as a result of oral transmission.
61. Stith Thompson, *The Folktale* (New York: Dryden Press, 1951), p. 448.
62. Lauri Honko, "Methods in Folk-Narrative Research," *Ethnologia Europaea* 11 (1979–1980): 8, remarks that Krohn's dream of such an *Urform* as the "most legitimate target of all folkloristic research has been abandoned long ago."
63. Christine Goldberg makes this statement in her survey of the results of the historic-geographic method. The statement represents Jason's final point of her summary of the Russian criticism of the Finnish method's achievements. Goldberg contends that the statement is not true, but she is able to adduce little hard evidence to refute it. See Goldberg, "The

Historic-Geographic Method," pp. 8–12; and Jason, "Structural Analysis," p. 291.

64. For the concept of oicotype coined by von Sydow, see his "Geography and Folk-Tale Oicotypes," in *Selected Papers on Folklore*, pp. 44–59. For additional discussion of the concept, see Laurits Bødker, *Folk Literature (Germanic)* (Copenhagen: Rosenkilde and Bagger, 1965), p. 220; Lauri Honko, "The Formation of Ecotypes," in Nikolai Burlakoff and Carl Lindahl, eds., *Folklore on Two Continents: Essays in Honor of Linda Dégh*, (Bloomington: Trickster Press, 1980), pp. 280–85; or Honko's earlier discussion "Traditional Barriers and Adaptation of Tradition," *Ethnologia Scandinavica: A Journal for Nordic Ethnology* (1973): 30–49. See also Linda-May Ballard, "The Formulation of the Oicotype: A Case Study," *Fabula* 24 (1983): 233–45; and Timothy Cochrane, "The Concept of Ecotypes in American Folklore," *Journal of Folklore Research* 24 (1987): 33–55.

65. Oscar Lewis, "Comparisons in Cultural Anthropology," p. 260. It should be noted that there is an even more voluminous literature devoted to the comparative method in sociology. See, for example, Edward A. Suchman, "The Comparative Method in Social Research," *Rural Sociology* 29 (1964): 123–37; Neil J. Smelser, *Comparative Methods in the Social Sciences* (Englewood Cliffs, N.J.: Prentice-Hall, 1976); and Charles C. Ragin, "Comparative Sociology and the Comparative Method," *International Journal of Comparative Sociology* 22 (1981): 102–20. See also Gideon Sjoberg, "The Comparative Method in the Social Sciences," *Philosophy of Science* 22 (1955): 106–17.

66. For Frazer's principles of sympathetic magic, see his discussion of "The Roots of Magic," in Sir James Frazer, *The New Golden Bough*, ed. by Theodor H. Gaster (New York: Mentor, 1964), pp. 35–70.

67. For van Gennep's brilliant analysis of rites (rites of separation, threshold rites, and rites of aggregation or readmission) see *The Rites of Passage* (Chicago: University of Chicago Press, 1960). I would take issue with Nicole Belmont in her book *Arnold van Gennep: The Creator of French Ethnography* (Chicago: University of Chicago Press, 1979), pp. 10, 132, when she insists that van Gennep was a weak or poor theoretician. How many anthropologists or folklorists have contributed as much to "theory" as van Gennep?

68. For an illustration of this form of the comparative method in folkloristic analysis, see Alan Dundes, *Life Is Like a Chicken Coop Ladder: A Portrait of German Culture Through Folklore* (New York: Columbia University Press, 1984).

69. It is encouraging to observe that the nature of the comparative method in folkloristics continues to be debated. Essays such as Helge Gerndt, "Vergleichende Volkskunde. Zur Bedeutung des Vergleichs in der volkskundlichen Methodik," *Zeitschrift für Volkskunde* 68 (1972) 179–95; Karel Horálek, "O teoretické základy folklórní komparatistiky"

[The theoretical basis of folkloristic comparative studies], *Česky Lid* 64 (1977): 205–11; Oldrich Sirovatka, "Otázky a úkoly srovnávací folkloristiky" [Questions and tasks of comparative folkloristics], *Slovenský Národopis* 25 (1977): 392–405, and Robert A. Georges, "The Folklorist as Comparatist," *Western Folklore* 45 (1986): 1–20, suggest that there is still considerable interest in the comparative method among professional folklorists.

Pecking Chickens: A Folk Toy as a Source for the Study of Worldview

No genre of folklore is so trivial or so insignificant that it cannot provide important data for the study of worldview. Worldview, the way a people perceives the world and its place in it, permeates all aspects of a given culture and this is why the pattern of the whole is to be found even in that whole's smallest part. Yet it is not always easy to discern patterns of worldview, especially when one attempts to look at a culture as a whole. Methodologically, it makes more sense to examine microcosms, and from these examinations, one may have better access to the corresponding macrocosm.

If one accepts the hypothesis that microcosms may be isomorphically parallel to macrocosms, then this might encourage folklorists to reconsider one of the oldest recorded genres of folklore: the folk toy. For toys are almost always miniatures, or "microspheres" to use Erikson's coinage,[1] of the "real" or adult world. Folk-toy research has not really sought to elucidate toys from this perspective, preferring instead merely to catalog toy specimens as found in a particular museum exhibition or to detail how to construct a specific toy.[2]

How might a folk toy be plausibly regarded as a model or metaphor or microcosm of the cultures in which it is found? Towards this goal, let us briefly discuss one of the standard wooden folk toys widespread in Europe and parts of Asia: the pecking chickens.

The pecking chickens toy consists of one or two or, more commonly, four wooden chickens sitting on a paddle-shaped platform. Underneath the platform is a weight of some kind which serves as a pendulum. The platform typically has a handle. When the handle is grasped, the platform is moved so that the weight rotates (either clockwise or counterclockwise). The head and/or neck of the chickens are jointed, and strings leading from each of the joints through holes in the platform connect the head/neck to the pendulum. While the chickens' bodies remain stationary, the heads of the chickens are forced downward in succession as the pendulum rotates. The faster the pendulum moves, the more rapidly the chickens peck. Often there is a representation of grain painted on the platform at which the chickens appear to peck. Characteristic of the toy is the clacking noise produced by the sounds of the chickens' beaks striking the platform. It is a relatively simple wooden construction and it seems to be listed in many of the standard surveys of folk toys.[3]

In the present context, I am not seeking to discover how old the pecking chickens toy might be. Nor am I interested in establishing the total overall distribution of the toy or in suggesting paths of possible diffusion of the toy from one culture to another. For my purposes, it is sufficient to state that the toy is found in such countries as China (Taiwan), Czechoslovakia, East Germany, England, India, Italy, Poland, Spain, Sweden, the Soviet Union, and the United States of America, among others.

For the past decade or so (1970–85), I have made a conscious effort to purchase exemplars of the toy in various gift shops and toystores in different parts of the world. Students and colleagues knowing of my interest have generously sent me specimens when they have come upon them in tourist or novelty shops.[4] Most of the toys indicate where they were made, e.g., "made in Taiwan," "made in Poland," and I have accepted these indications as reliable markers of provenience. The majority seem to be of recent fabrication and in fact are apparently produced as a form of "folk art" to be sold to tourists.

From these several dozen examples of the pecking chickens, I propose to draw certain inferences. For the record, I willingly acknowledge that it is dangerous to generalize on the basis of so few "texts," so to speak, but from a structural perspective, even a single text so long as it is truly representative (and admittedly representativeness, in the absence of numerous versions from the same

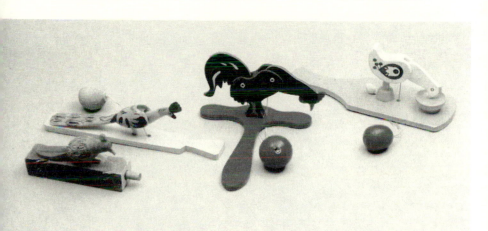

Figure 1. *Left to right:*
Russian, Russian, English, and Italian versions.

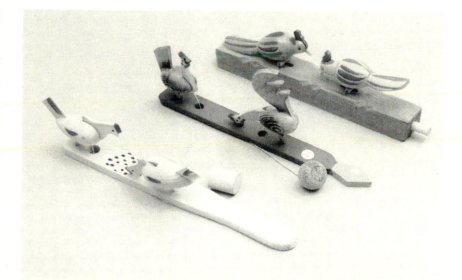

Figure 2. *Left to right:* Czech, Polish, and Russian chickens.

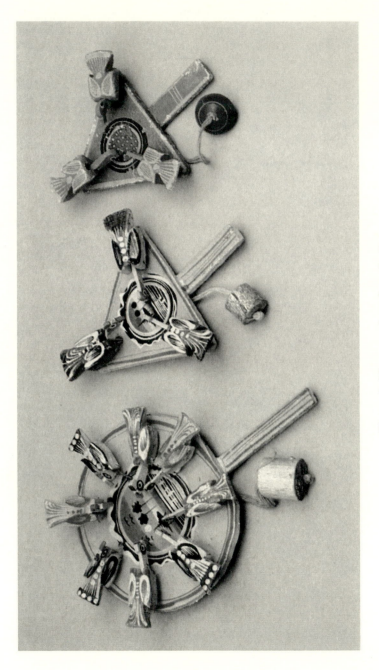

Figure 3. Three versions from India.

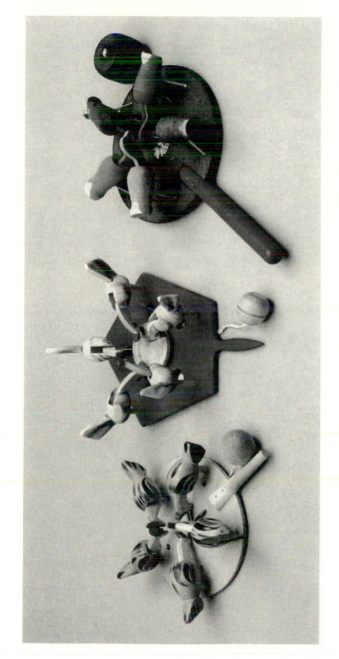

Figure 4. *Left to right*: Russian, Polish, and Taiwanese chickens.

Figure 5. Three versions from the United States.

Figure 6. *Left to right, top:* From East Germany and Sweden.
Left to right, bottom: From Spain and the Soviet Union.

culture, can only be assumed rather than demonstrated) can be utilized to yield data about cultural patterning. Specifically, I shall try to suggest how perceptions of personal space and food supply can be reflected in the details of any one instance of the pecking chickens. What I hope to show is that each pecking chickens toy represents in miniature something of the folk's conception of the nature of the world in which they live.

Without a full-fledged historic-geographic, comparative study of the pecking chickens, one cannot ascertain oicotypes, that is, local forms of the toy which reflect unique and distinctive national or regional characteristics which differ from features of the toy found elsewhere.[5] However, I believe the comparative data to be presented will allow some oicotypical hypotheses to be formulated. It is oicotypes (rather than subtypes, which are not necessarily restricted to one given national or cultural context) which offer the greatest potential for the identification of possible national (or regional) character traits. I want to stress that I am not so much concerned with the validity of the generalizations I intend to make (though I am personally persuaded of their accuracy). Rather I want to document a potential methodology which might fruitfully be applied to other folk toys, not to mention material culture objects generally.

It is not entirely clear just how old the pecking chickens toy is. We find, for example, that Carl Martin Plümicke (1749–1833) in his *Briefe aus einer Reise durch Deutschland im Jahr 1791*, published in 1793, provides a list of wooden toys he observed, and one of those specifically mentioned is pecking chickens.[6] It is highly likely that the toy is much older, and we may regard 1791 strictly as a provisional *terminus ante quem*. In any event, the concern in this investigation is not with documenting the undoubted antiquity of the pecking chickens.

The examples of pecking chickens I have assembled from a dozen different countries manifest multiple existence and variation, the two criteria which constitute the *sine qua non* of authentic folklore. No two examples are exactly alike, and it is quite fascinating to see the variation in such features as the shape and thickness of the paddle-platform, the size and dimensions of the pendulum, the number, design, and color of the chicken figures, the symbolic representation of the food supply, etc. Generally speaking, I assume the examples are cognate in the sense that we are dealing with a common traditional toy. While it could in theory have been invented twice, it seems more likely that we have here instances of toymakers in one country imitating a toy observed in or imported from another country.

To be sure, the inevitable debate over the merits of monogenesis and diffusion over polygenesis as championed by most folklorists is never absolutely convincing. Still, the limited evidence available does point to a possible single origin even if we cannot ascertain with accuracy the place and date of that presumed original pecking chickens prototype.

A few pecking chickens toys occur in the form of one single chicken sitting on a relatively limited rectangularly shaped platform (Figure 1, Russian, Russian, English, Italian). The first of the four illustrations of a single pecking chicken, from the Soviet Union, depends upon a principle other than the more usual pendulum. In this case, a cylindrical piece of wooden doweling fits into a round hole in the platform block. Pushing the protruding portion of the doweling into the block forces the head of the bird down onto the platform, while releasing the doweling (which is attached to a simple spring mechanism) allows the bird's head to return to an upright position. This technique is also commonly found in a wooden bear toy popular in the Soviet Union. The second of this series, also from the Soviet Union, employs the pendulum. In this instance, the bird represented seems to be a peacock. The third exemplar, from England, is a large colorful rooster. The fourth, from Italy, is the only specimen I have where an egg is displayed. One is tempted to speculate about the importance of the mother and child configuration (as suggested by the chicken and egg) in Italian culture.[7]

Another variant form of the toy consists of two chickens facing one another (Figure 2, Czech, Polish, Russian). We may remark here how the chickens peck in alternate sequence. The Czech version includes a random assortment of twenty-two dots painted on the platform representing the food supply for the chickens; the Polish version has no representation of food whatsoever—the chickens peck well enough but to no purpose; while the Russian dowel-spring variant displays five rows of nine tiny square empty indentations standing presumably for a food source, though one might argue that they show merely the places where the birds' beaks have sought in vain for food.

The most common form of the pecking chickens toy has more than one or two birds. Typically there are four and five chickens pecking, though some variants have more and some fewer. The occurrence of that many chickens sharing a common platform permits a comparison of both space and food allocation as displayed in different cultures. In theory, all of the chickens could have been constructed with the same amount of symbolic food available—how much trouble is it to paint dots on a wooden base? Similarly, all of the chickens could have been given the same amount of "personal" space within which to search for food. Yet, as we shall observe, there are dramatic differences with respect to the availability of individual space and food from one toy exemplar (and the society in which it was fabricated) to another. I am not suggesting that the toymaker was consciously commenting upon food and space as commodities in his culture. Quite the contrary, it is far more likely that toymakers in a given society construct toys in accordance with unstated worldview premises consonant with the similar worldview principles of their prospective consumers. In effect, these unstated premises are articulated through the medium of the folk toy. Moreover, the remarkable differences in cultural perceptions of food and space allowances become apparent only in the light of comparison. The comparative method is absolutely critical for the delineation of possible oicotypes.

In three versions of the toy from India (Figure 3), we may note that only one has any representation of food, as symbolized as dots contained within a circular area in the center of the triangular platform. The other two versions offer a pretty picture instead of food. It is almost as though art or cosmology were presumed to be a worthy substitute for food. (The penchant for art seemingly has analogs in body decoration and costume design in India.) In one Indic version, there are some eight birds pecking at the large painted picture, a number which may well hint at a basic overpopulation problem in that part of the world as well as the corresponding difficulties in providing food for such large populations.

We find similar clues in examples from the Soviet Union, Poland, and Taiwan (Figure 4). The Russian chickens' heads are close to one another as they peck, and there is only the barest hint of food. The Polish chickens have slightly more headroom, but they are shown pecking from one single communal bowl, a bowl which appears to be entirely empty. The five Taiwanese chickens have so little individual headroom that it is virtually impossible for all the heads to peck at once—if the pendulum allowed them to do so, which it does not. At least some white rock fragments, possibly representing rice, pasted to the platform suggest food is available.

We may contrast these with three versions of the toy from the United States (Figure 5). The American exemplars are the only ones, to my knowledge, to use actual food. Kernels of corn are glued to the wooden platforms. Typically each chicken has his own individual corn kernel to peck at. The glaring difference between the life-size real corn kernels and the miniaturized scale of the abstract wooden chickens serves to emphasize the physical bulk and presence of food. Only a country with an abundant food supply could waste food to construct or decorate a toy. ("Chicken feed" in American slang refers to something of little monetary value.) It is a sad indictment of the world's distribution of resources when one country uses corn kernels to adorn a toy while other countries are devastated by famine. Also worth noting in the American versions are the massive, thick platforms and rugged chickens. In the third of these, from Columbia, California, which was a center for gold mining activity in the mid-nineteenth century, the pendulum consists of a rock painted gold. Thus, it is a gold weight which allows the American chickens to enjoy their individual kernels of corn.

As a final comparison of the pecking chickens, we may consider versions from East Germany, Sweden, the Soviet Union, and Spain (Figure 6). The East German chickens peck at a round green sward which has no apparent food; The Swedish version, which is a commercially produced one (by Brio), has the most food of any example of the toy. There are too many dots to count. Yet the yellow Swedish chickens are all identical, which hints at some degree of conformity—even if personal space and food are relatively abundant. To be sure, it may be that it is the commercialization of the toy which accounts for the common color of the chickens. Presumably it is easier and cheaper to have all the chickens the same color. The five Russian chickens have no color at all (though in most Russian versions, the chickens display handsome red and black coloration—cf. Figure 4). Again, they enjoy very little individual headroom and they have no food. The three Spanish chickens are individually decorated and they have a sufficient food supply well encircled. If we were to risk a comparison of just these four versions of the pecking chickens with respect to perceptions of food supply, we could remark that the Russian chickens have no food; the East Germans have the space (green turf) for food, but none is available; the Spanish chickens have some food, but there is a finite number of food dots and it is bounded by a green circle; while the Swedish chickens have an unbounded and near infinite amount of food. If we consider these same four specimens in terms of personal space, we can easily see that the Swedish chickens have the most space; the Spanish chickens have the next most space available per individual; the East Germans have enough space theoretically for all three chickens to peck at the same time; the Russian chickens have the least space.

We must reiterate our initial caution that it is dangerous to speculate on the basis of too few texts or exemplars. Can we be sure that the versions of pecking chickens described here are truly representative? Moreover, we are dealing with symbolic delineations of food and space, not concrete detailed statistical surveys of housing availability or food supplies. Nevertheless, even if these pecking chickens provide only *perceptions* of food and space availability, they are valuable clues to such perceptions. Worldview, a people's perception of the world, is often difficult to grasp. People cannot always articulate worldview principles to inquiring ethnographers and folklorists any more than they can articulate principles of the grammar of their native language. Yet just as languages are governed by inducible principles so worldviews are equally highly patterned. While it has been customary to seek to extrapolate worldview principles from such exalted elements of culture as cosmogonies and mythology, it would also seem possible if not extremely practical to discern such principles from more humble cultural artifacts. For in the particle we may find the same patterning as in the whole. If this is so, then folklorists may wish to examine folk toys as a potential and virtually untapped rich source for the study of worldview.

NOTES

1. See Erik H. Erikson, "Toys and Reasons" in *Childhood and Society*, 2nd ed. (New York: W.W. Norton, 1963), 221.

2. For an entrée into the considerable literature devoted to collections of folk toys, see folklorist Robert Wildhaber's valuable bibliographical addendum to the *Kinderspielzug* catalog which served as a guide for an exhibit held jointly by the Museum für Völkerkunde and the Schweizerische Museum für Volkskunde in Basel from December, 1964, to April, 1965.

3. According to Emanuel Hercík, *Folk Toys* (Prague: Orbis, 1951), 25, "Pecking hens are still made as toys in various places in Bohemia and in the neighbourhood of Myjava and Stará Turá in Slovakia." For an illustration in color, see plate 73. For another account of the versions of pecking chickens in Slovakia, see Pavol Michalides, *L'udové Hračky na Slovensku* (Bratislava: Vydavatel'stvo Slovenskej Vied, 1972), 113, 122–23. In an account of "Toys of the London Pavements," we are told of "Wooden hens, bobbing after grain at the swinging of a weight." See Lesley Gordon, *Peepshow into Paradise: A History of Children's Toys* (New York: John De Graff, 1953), 75. One can find the toy cited or pictured in various collections, e.g., of Russian wooden toys, but the accounts are strictly descriptive with no attempt at analysis.

4. There are too many individuals for me to thank by name, but I must acknowledge my indebtedness to folklorist Pam Ow, who not only purchased examples of the toy in various shops in the United States, but also located illustrations of the toy in several published collections of folk art. I must also thank Gene Prince, photographer for the R. H. Lowie Museum of Anthropology at the University of California, Berkeley, for the splendid pictures which accompany this essay.

5. For the concept of oicotype, originally coined by Swedish folklorist C.W. von Sydow in 1927, see Laurits Bødker, *Folk Literature (Germanic)* (Copenhagen: Rosenkilde and Bagger, 1965), 220, and Lauri Honko, "The Formation of Ecotypes," in *Folklore on Two Continents: Essays in Honor of Linda Dègh*, eds. Nikolai Burlakoff & Carl Lindahl (Bloomington: Trickster Press, 1980), 280–85. See also Honko's earlier discussion of the concept of oicotype in his "Traditional Barriers and Adaptation of Tradition," *Ethnologia Scandinavica: A Journal for Nordic*

Ethnology 1973: 30–49, and Timothy Cochrane, "The Concept of Eco-types in American Folklore," *Journal of Folklore Research* 24 (1987), 33–55.

6. See Karl Ewald Fritzsch and Manfred Bachmann, *An Illustrated History of Toys* (London: Abbey Library, 1965), 29.

7. For an extended discussion of an example of the mother-and-child constellation in Italian culture, see Alan Dundes and Alessandro Falassi, *La Terra in Piazza: An Interpretation of the Palio of Siena* (Berkeley and Los Angeles: University of California Press, 1975), 199–218.

On Whether Weather "Proverbs" Are Proverbs

Traditional sayings about the weather, wise or otherwise, have commonly but wrongly been considered proverbs by folklorists for more than a century. A host of titles attests to the purported existence of weather proverbs. Reinsberg-Düringsfeld published *Das Wetter im Sprichwort* in 1864; Richard Inwards, *Weather Lore: A Collection of Proverbs, Sayings and Rules Concerning the Weather* appeared in 1869; and Rev. Charles Swainson, *A Handbook of Weather Folk-Lore: Being A Collection of Proverbial Sayings in Various Languages Relating to the Weather* in 1873. Other sources include C. W. Empson, "Weather Proverbs and Sayings Not Contained in Inwards' or Swainson's Books," *Folklore Record* 4 (1881), 126–132; Alexis Yermoloff's comprehensive *Die landwirtschaftliche Volksweisheit in Sprichwörtern, Redensarten und Wetterregein* (1905); and William J. Humphreys, *Weather Proverbs and Paradoxes* (1923).

Standard surveys of the proverb genre include mention of so-called weather proverbs. F. Edward Hulme concluded his *Proverb Lore* (1902) with a discussion of weather proverbs (pp. 264–269); Archer Taylor devotes a substantial section of *The Proverb* (1931) to weather proverbs (pp. 109–121); Röhrich and Mieder in *Sprichwort* (1977) list "Wettersprichwort (Bauern-regel)" as their first example of special forms of proverbs (pp. 7–10). Articles on weather proverbs have even appeared in *Proverbium*, e.g., Nai-tung Ting, "Chinese Weather Proverbs," *Proverbium* 18 (1972), 649–655 which would suggest at least tacit acceptance of this sub-generic category. Wolfgang Mieder's superb *International Proverb*

Scholarship (1982) contains more than forty references to collections or discussions of weather proverbs.

From this admittedly cursory bibliographical survey, one can safely surmise that 'weather proverbs' constitute a legitimate subtype of the proverb genre and further that the study of them falls appropriately under the rubric of paremiology. I believe this is a generic error and that what are commonly called weather proverbs are nothing more than superstitions. What has tended to confuse folklorists is that whereas superstitions are more often than not free phrase, weather superstitions frequently occur in rhymed fixed-phrase form. In other words, they are superstitions with the textural features of proverbs (and riddles). It is likely that these textural features are present for mnemonic purposes. It is easier to remember a fact if it is couched in rhyme. The point, however, is that a rhymed superstition is still a superstition, *not* a proverb.

Let us take a representative instance. There is a venerable folk belief that a red sky in the evening signals fair weather to follow while a red sky in the morning predicts bad weather. Two distinct "proverbs" based on this belief are to be found in *The Oxford Dictionary of English Proverbs*, Third Edition (1970). They are: Sky red in the morning is a sailor's (shepherd's) warning; sky red at night is the sailor's (shepherd's) delight. Evening red and morning grey help the traveller on his way; evening grey and morning red bring down rain upon his head.

This is an old tradition going back as many have observed to a New Testament version (Matthew 16:2–3): "When it is evening, ye say, it will be fair weather: for the sky is red. And in the morning, it will be foul weather today: for the sky is red and lowering." The Biblical text provides a useful *terminus ante quem* for this belief which is one of the numerous weather sayings which has been tested by meteorologists and found to be relatively accurate.[1]

Frick in an important four-part study of traditional weather predictions which appeared in the *Schweizerisches Archiv für Volkskunde* in 1926 delineated what is essentially a structural definition of such items. According to Frick, they inevitably consist of "présages (a), date des présages (b), pronostics (c), and échéance (d)."[2] Another "proverb" contained in the *Oxford Dictionary of English Proverbs*, "April showers bring forth May flowers" can serve to illustrate Frick's pattern. The sign (a) would be showers, the date of the sign (b) would be April, the prognostication (c) would be flowers, and the date of the prognostication (d) would be May. The "Red sky at night, Shepherd's (Sailor's) delight" text would fit the same pattern. From a folkloristic perspective, this is clearly a sign superstition.[3] If A, then B. If there is a red sky in the evening, there will be good weather next day. If there is a red sky in the morning, bad weather is imminent. This superstition, *like all superstitions*, is to be interpreted *literally*. True *proverbs*, in contrast, are nearly always to be understood *metaphorically*.

The red sky in the evening is never used metaphorically. It is always a literal weather sign superstition. Even Jesus, according to Matthew (16:1–4), understood this tradition correctly as a sign. It is folklorists who have mislabelled it as a proverb.

Sometimes superstitions do play on metaphors, but in those instances, they are interpreted literally. For example, if you carry a baby up a flight of stairs, you will ensure that he will rise in life. This magic superstition involves a literalization of a metaphor, namely, acting out a "rising" bit of behavior. Through homeopathic magic, a baby in an "upwardly mobile" society is given a superstitious boost by his or her parents. The theoretical issue with respect to whether a given text is a proverb or a superstition depends upon the literal/metaphorical distinction. We may best observe this by contrasting specific texts which can serve as either superstitions or proverbs!

"Lightning never strikes twice (in the same place)" is a superstition if it is understood to be a *literal* statement about the nature of lightning. If, for example, in a lightning storm, an individual sought refuge next to a charred tree stump previously struck by a lightning bolt, on the assumption that he would be safe (because lightning never strikes twice), we would be dealing with a superstitious belief. If, on the other hand, the same statement was understood *metaphorically* as used by individual A to individual B to assure or reassure B that a particular danger or unfortunate event could not possibly recur, then we would have a proverb.[4] Note that from the text alone we could not determine genre in this instance. We need context and interpretation before the generic category is clear. (This also suggests that structural analysis by itself without reference to context is insufficient to distinguish genre.)

In the same way, if "One swallow does not make a summer" is understood as a sign that the appearance of a single swallow (as opposed to a whole flock of swallows) means that summer (warmer weather) has not yet arrived, we have a weather superstition.[5] But if it is understood metaphorically as referring to the notion that one instance is inadequate evidence to support a particular generalization, then we have a proverb. Or if one refers to the "calm before the storm" as a literal period of tranquility signalling the approach of a thunderstorm, one has a superstition; if it refers metaphorically to a forthcoming argument or battle, it is a proverb.

Although superstitions are always literal, proverbs are not always metaphorical. One can cite a few literal proverbs (sometimes called aphorisms or maxims), e.g., "Honesty is the best policy." But the vast majority of true proverbs are demonstrably metaphorical insofar as they can be legitimately applied to a whole series of contexts and situations. Weather sayings to the extent that they are literal fall under the generic rubric of superstition. Most are sign superstitions. I believe the German scholarly tradition of referring to weather sayings as rules (Bauernregel) is far more accurate than referring to them as proverbs, but that designation still tends to mask their identity as bonafide superstitions.

What this means is that there are numerous texts included in the *Dictionary of English Proverbs*, and no doubt other standard collections of proverbs as well, which do not belong to the proverb genre at all. For example, in England, in the spring of 1983, I collected a number of versions of "One for sorrow, two for joy; three for a girl, four for a boy" which is allegedly recited upon sighting one or more magpies. A longer form is found in the *Dictionary of English Proverbs* which begins "One [magpie] for sorrow; two for mirth; three for a wedding: four for a birth. . . ." A female informant explained to me that inasmuch as magpies tended to cluster in pairs, the rhyme had sexist overtones—boys (four magpies) were more likely than girls (three magpies).[6] The very structure of the rhyme would tend to support such an assertion to the extent that sorrow and girls are aligned in contrast to joys and boys. Whatever the chauvinist implications of the text may be, it is clearly a form of divination. Hence it belongs to the genre of superstition (where there are many signs of whether a future baby will be a boy or a girl). The fact that it is in rhyme does not make it any the less a sign superstition. It is not a proverb.

With similar reasoning, I would argue that most of what proverb scholars have referred to as "medical proverbs," e.g., An apple a day keeps the doctor away,[7] are simply rhymed folk medical superstitions. If A, then B. If one eats an apple daily, one will be healthy. Finally, I do not really believe that the folk consider weather and medical rules as proverbs. It is rather the folklorists who have wrongly constructed such erroneous classificatory categories. To the original question raised: Are weather proverbs proverbs? I would say emphatically "No!"

NOTES

1. See, for example, Spencer Russell, "A Red Sky at Night . . ." *Meteorological Magazine*, 61 (1926), 15–17, and Paul J. Marriott, *Red Sky at Night, Shepherd's Delight? Weather Lore of the English Countryside* (Oxford: Sheba Books, 1981), pp. 309–311. For representative discussions of the scientific merit of such weather signs, see Georges Tibau, "Zestig Vlaamse weerspreuken onder de loep van de statistiek," *Volkskunde* 78 (1977), 33–59; and M. G. Wurtele, "Some Thoughts on Weather Lore," *Folklore* 82 (1971), 292–303.

2. See R.-O Frick, "Le peuple et la prévision du temps," *Schweizerisches Archiv für Volkskunde*, 26 (1926), 1–21, 89–100, 171–188, 254–279. For the structural formula, see pp. 5–6. See also Eleanor Anne Forster, *The Proverb and Superstition Defined*. Diss. University of Pennsylvania, 1968.

3. For a discussion of the definition of sign superstitions, see Alan Dundes, "Brown County Superstitions," *Midwest Folklore*, II (1961), 25–56 (see esp. pp. 28–31). The theoretical portion of this essay was reprinted in Alan Dundes, *Analytic Essays in Folklore* (The Hague: Mouton, 1975), pp. 88–94.

4. Ronald Baker makes a similar case in "'Hogs Are Playing with Sticks—Bound to Be Bad Weather': Folk Belief or Proverb?" *Midwestern Journal of Language and Folklore*, I (1975): 65–67; reprinted in *Readings*

in American Folklore, ed. Jan Harold Brunvand (New York: W. W. Norton, 1979), pp. 199–202.

5. Marriott, *op. cit.*, pp. III, 159, claims the saying is true "because at the end of March and during April they arrive in ones and twos, only coming in force from mid to late April."

6. Ms. Elizabeth Fassett, a student enrolled in my introductory folklore course at the University of California, Berkeley, in the fall semester of 1988, collected a striking Irish text of the magpie formula:

> One for sorrow
> Two for joy
> Three for a girl
> Four for a boy
> Five for silver
> Six for gold
> Seven for a secret never to be told
> Eight's a wish
> Nine's a kiss
> Ten's a bird you must not miss

Her female informant explained that it was very bad luck to see just one magpie, but that one could get rid of the bad luck caused thereby either by spitting and saluting the solitary bird or by making someone else look at the bird. In the latter case, it is the person tricked into looking at the single magpie who receives the first person's bad luck instead. Apparently, in Ireland it becomes almost a game to try to force a second person to notice the magpie. It should be remarked that the sexist bias in the alternated lines continues as gold (aligned with joy and boy) is presumably more valuable than silver (aligned with sorrow and girl). Moreover, a girl is linked with not being allowed to tell a secret while a boy gets a wish.

7. This and other examples of medical "proverbs" may be found in Archer Taylor, *The Proverb* (Cambridge: Harvard University Press, 1931), pp. 121–129.

April Fool and April Fish:
Towards a Theory of Ritual Pranks

The study of humor includes the study of jokes. The study of jokes includes the study of practical jokes and yet anthropologists and folklorists have tended to neglect the subject of practical jokes or pranks.

In Europe, pranks are customarily associated with special days, especially April 1st. In the United States, pranks are played on April Fools' day as well as on Halloween. Also pranks are commonly a major component of traditional hazing or initiation ceremonies. Charivari, a custom whereby newlyweds are subjected to various practical jokes or indignities by the family or entire village community, provides another ritual occasion for prank behavior.

Typically on the first of April, a gullible victim, often a child, may be sent on a so-called fool's errand or "wild goose chase" as it is sometimes termed in American argot. Corso (1920:58, quoted in Basile 1950:113) remarks that the quest objects are diverse "e di esistenza impossibile, inverosimile, chimerica". Sometimes the false quest objects are localized by occupation. So a carpenter's apprentice might be sent for a board-stretcher (or in some versions, a board-shortener); a painter for a bucket of striped paint, a mechanic for a left-handed monkey wrench. A fledgling nurse's aide might be directed to find a Fallopian tube. Other traditional fools' errands include pigeon milk, elbow grease, a bucket of steam, etc.. In the mid-nineteenth century, a Norwegian version of the custom involved sending children on April 1st to the neighbors to borrow some warmth out of a bed (Christiansen 1947:129). (For lists of fools' errands, see Jungbauer 1927:559; Janssens 1958:107–08; Opie and Opie 1959:246).

The custom of indulging in pranks on April 1st is fairly wide-spread in Europe. The bulk of the entry on "April" in the *Handwörterbuch des Deutschen Aberglaubens* (Jungbauer 1927) documents the practice in Germany, France, England, Poland, Portugal, and Russia, among other countries. The name of the fool varies in different regions. For example, in several Romance language-speaking countries, notably France and Italy, the term April Fish is preferred (*poisson d'Avril, pesce d'Aprile*). A survey in the Sudentenland, the German-speaking part of northern Czechoslovakia, on the other hand, refers to the foolish individual sent on an April errand as *April-narr, April-ochse, April-kalb, April-esel, April-gans,* and *April-affe* (Wolf-Beranek 1968: 225–26).

In Scotland, the victim is known as a "Gowk" or cuckoo, and there are several traditional rhymes employing this term:

On the first of April
Send the gowk whither you will (Wight 1927:38).

In one version, the poor dupe is sent somewhere with a written message which reads:

Don't you laugh, and don't you smile
Hunt the gowk another mile (Opie and Opie 1959:245).

In this instance, the person who receives the message reads it, and then informs the dupe that the message has been brought to the wrong place and that it must be taken to someone else.

Actually one finds that traditional rhymes are often an integral part of April 1st pranks. Usually they serve to mock the victims, informing them that they have been the victims of a prank. In Geneva, in the nineteenth century, the following rhyme might be addressed to the dupe:

Mois d'avril
Qui fait courir
Les ânes gris
Jusqu'à Paris (Pitrè 1902:7).

A German rhyme refers not to gray donkeys racing to Paris, but to a piece of (s)catology:

April, April
De Katt schitt, wat se will (Jungbauer 1927:561).

This is presumably a variant of such rhymes as:

April, April
Kann 'n schicken wen 'n will (Pitrè 1902:19).

or:

Heute ist der erste April
Schickt man den Esel wo man will (Pitrè 1902:20).

For more details of the custom in particular countries, one may consult accounts in Belgium (Lemoine 1889; Janssens 1958); England (Opie and Opie 1959:243–47; Wight 1927); France (Sébillot 1888); French Canada (Laliberté 1980); Germany (Müller 1923/1924); Italy (Pitrè 1902; Corso 1920); Norway (Christiansen 1947) and Tripoli (Basile 1950), among others.

Despite the considerable number of essays devoted to April Fool and April Fish customary pranks, the tradition is not well understood. What function does the April fool prank serve? And why are pranks associated specifically with the first of April?

The Grimm brothers mentioned the custom in the first volume of their famous *Deutsches Wörterbuch* in 1854: "der brauch, unserm alterthum unbekannt, scheint uns erst in der letzten jhh. dort seinem ursprung nach unaufgeklärt, jedenfalls hängt er mit dem beginn des neuen jahrs im april zusammen" (1854:538). The possible French origin of the custom was also suggested by Giuseppe Pitrè of Sicily. Pitrè, the first major folklorist to consider the prank in any depth, wrote a sixteen-page pamphlet in 1886 entitled " 'Il pesce d'Aprile". By 1891, there was a fifth edition of some 29 pages "con moltissime giunte". Later, Pitrè published an expanded version of this influential essay as the first chapter of a book *Curiosità di usi popolari* (1902:1–51). He remarked "E difficile trovare nel campo delle tradizioni popolari un uso, la cui origine sia tanto oscura e controversa quanto questa del pesce d'Aprile" (1902:23). More than one hundred years of scholarship has unfortunately added very little to our knowledge and understanding of this curious custom. Laliberté observes that the custom's significance and origin remain obscure (1980:79). A folk rhyme which has existed from at least as early as 1760 expresses the same bewilderment:

> The first of April some do say,
> Is set apart for All Fools' Day;
> But why the people call it so
> Nor I, nor they themselves, do know
> But on that day are people sent
> On purpose for pure merriment (Christiansen 1947:131).

The custom does go back at least to the early sixteenth century. It is mentioned in a 1508 French source (Rosières 1892:196; Laliberté 1980:82). According to one source, the first known occurrence in Germany was in 1618 (Wolf-Beranek 1968:233), but ultimate origins are almost always impossible to ascertain definitively.

The few theories purporting to explain the custom are pretty far fetched. Most are heavily tinged with Christian or biblical bias as is one suggestion that "poisson" (as in "poisson d'Avril") was nothing more than a corruption of the "passion" of Jesus on the cross (Sébillot 1884:185; Pitrè 1902:25; Janssens 1958:110; cf. Laliberté 1980:81). As Rosières (1892:195) aptly observed, it is highly doubtful that this hypothesis ever satisfied anyone. Another "Christian" theory proposed that the fruitless or impossible errand was intended to be a parody of Christ being sent from Pilate to Herod and from Herod to Pilate (Pitrè 1902:24; Janssens 1958:109). This too seems highly unlikely. Yet another dubious theory which goes back at least to 1769 (Eichler 1924:414–415) claimed that the April fool custom commemorated the flight of Noah's dove from the ark before the waters had abated. "Her errand was a bootless one and occurred (the tradition says) on April 1, but the custom of April fooling was set up (we are told) for the pious purpose of commemorating the memory of Noah's deliverance from the ark" (Pitrè 1902:25,n.2).

Various theories have been proposed by French folklorists seeking to explicate the "fish" element of the custom, but none are convincing. Most probably the term refers to fish being "caught". One of the obvious functions of pranks is to "catch" the dupe or victim. In Italian, supposedly a fish is a slang term for a simpleton or a fool (Janssens 1958:111). One of the more novel older interpretations of the custom was proposed by Angelo de Gubernatis in his *Zoological Mythology*. According to de Gubernatis, "The fish is a phallic symbol (in the Neapolitan dialect, *pesce*, fish, is the phallos itself" (1872:249; cf. Christiansen 1947:132–33). He continues (1872:250) "The joke of the April fish (*le poisson d'Avril*), with which so many of our ladies ingenuously amuse themselves, has a scandalously phallical signification". This interpretation may cast some light on a custom practiced in Holland, for example, wherein a paper herring may be affixed to the back of some victim's clothes (Jungbauer 1927:559).

In order to better understand the April Fool custom of playing pranks, we might first consider the nature of the prank genre in general. The term "practical joke" in English suggests that there is a semantic connection between prank and verbal joke. A practical joke, however, implies that the joke is *not* a verbal one, but rather one which involves action or activity of some kind. Nevertheless, like a verbal joke, a practical joke involves a butt or dupe or victim. Jokes are almost always at someone's expense (even if it is just the joketeller himself). This is unquestionably the case with practical jokes. There must be a prankster (corresponding to the trickster in trickster tales) and a gullible dupe. In addition, one finds that there is typically an audience, often consisting of the prankster's peers, present to enjoy the prank. The audience frequently joins in to assist with the eventual humiliation of the victim. There is very often a severe streak of sadism and cruelty in traditional pranks, a fact conveniently overlooked by the prankster and his associates. Occasionally, a victim of bodily harm has sought legal redress of his grievances (cf. Reynolds 1984).

One of the relatively few attempts to define the practical joke was made by folklorist Richard S. Tallman in his essay "A Generic Approach to the Practical Joke" which was part of a special issue of *Southern Folklore Quarterly* devoted to the genre (Tallman 1974):

> The practical joke, as a folklore form, is first an event, a competitive play activity in which only one of two opposing sides is consciously aware of the fact that a state of play exists; for the joke to be successful, one side must remain unaware of the fact that a play activity is occurring until it is "too late", that is, until the unknowing side is made to

seem foolish or is caused some physical and/or mental discomfort (1974:260).

Tallman goes on to distinguish between individual and group pranksters, between individual and groups of victims, the prank action, benevolent and malevolent pranks, and successful and unsuccessful pranks (1974:263–64).

It is true that the dupe or victim must be persuaded that fiction is fact, that falsehood is truth, in order for a prank or practical joke to succeed. Structurally speaking, initially a deceit is proposed by the prankster. If the dupe accepts the faulty premise and carries out the activity entailed by it, we have the second stage of deception. The last obligatory structural element is the revelation of the deception whereby the victim learns that he or she has been deceived.

Usually pranks are played upon individuals, but once in a while a whole group is duped. A newspaper, the *Evening Star*, announced on 31 March 1864 that a grand exhibition of donkeys would be held on the following day at the Agricultural Hall in Islington. Early on the morning of April 1st, a large crowd assembled outside the doors of the hall only to discover that they themselves were the donkeys (Wight 1927:40).

In distinguishing practical jokes from verbal jokes, we must also admit that some actual pranks become the subjects of traditional narratives. In some instances, it may be difficult to determine whether the pranks described in prank narratives ever actually occured. For example, various engineering schools in the United States (e.g., M.I.T. or Cal Tech) serve as the locale for a prank in which during a vacation period, a student's car is completely disassembled and then put back together inside his dormitory room. When the student returns from vacation, he is astonished to find his automobile parked in his room.

In a traditional American medical school prank story, several medical students crossing a toll bridge hold out of the car window a cadaver's arm (which they have illegally removed from the dissecting laboratory). In the outstretched hand of the cadaver is the money required to pay the toll. In some versions, the toll-booth attendant's hair turns white; in others, he dies of a heart attack.

In one sense, it makes no difference whether the pranks actually occurred or not. The prank story itself can be subjected to content analysis. In the medical school legend, it has been suggested that medical students need to become totally familiar with cadavers (overcoming perhaps a revulsion for dealing with dead bodies). Moreover, they must also become sufficiently dispassionate to be able to pay their way through life by treating the sick and the dying without feeling overly remorseful and sad. In short, they must learn to become able to put the limbs and bodies of their dead patients aside, to leave them behind as it were, even as they use the money obtained from their patients to make their living. Through inversion, it is the outside world symbolized by the toll-booth attendant rather than the medical students who is shocked at the sight of taking money from the hands of the dead.

Most of the pranks reportedly played at boarding schools or summer camps (cf. Posen 1974) do occur. These would include putting bouillon cubes in the shower heads or placing a sleeping victim's hand into a basin or bucket of lukewarm water which is supposed to make the victim urinate in bed. The latter would appear to be a technique intended to infantilize the victim—by reducing him to a pre-toilet-trained baby who still wets his bed.

Defining pranks in terms of a structural sequence of (1) Deceit proposed by prankster, (2) Deception accepted by dupe, and (3) Revelation of deception, and giving examples of various pranks does not appear to illuminate the question of why pranks are associated specifically with the first of April. What rationale, if any, can be adduced to explain why pranks are played on that date?

In order to elucidate this puzzling custom, we need first to better understand the function of pranks generally and more importantly to investigate their contexts. If we extrapolate from all the most typical contexts for pranks, we can easily see that they occur most often to individuals *who are placed in some kind of new situation or status*. The key word is *new*. Pranks are played upon *new*comers to neighborhoods (Penich 1954), *new*lyweds, initiates in fraternities or sororities, *new* arrivals at a summer vacation camp or a boarding school (Posen 1974).

This is easy to document. One occasion for pranks is a newcomer's first day on a job. There is even a motif, J2346, Fool's errand. An apprentice, or newcomer or ignorant person, etc., is sent for absurd or misleading or nonexistent object or on a ridiculous quest. According to the *Motif-Index of Folk-Literature*, this is reported in Canada, England, and the United States (For Scotland, see Honeyman 1958/1959). One suspects that it has much wider distribution but that it has simply not been reported elsewhere. There is also motif J2347, occupational tricks on new employees. (The only reference cited for both motifs is Baughman 1966.)

It is not only newcomers to occupational groups who have pranks played upon them. The newcomers may be recent arrivals in a neighborhood or to a summer vacation camp. For example, in the latter context, new campers may be invited to go on a snipe hunt (Baughman motif J2349.6*) in which a dupe is told how to hunt snipe at night, snipe being either a bird or a small furry rodent. Typically, the novice takes a bag or sack plus a flashlight. In some versions of the prank, the flashlight is supposed to attract the attention of the snipe; in others, one uses the flashlight to blind the eyes of the snipe which causes them to fall down into the sack. Sometimes, the victim is required to call the snipe or to summon them by whistling or by making noise (banging pots and pans together). In some cases, the other members of the group go out and make noise, e.g., by beating the bushes, allegedly to flush out the snipe and herd them towards the unsuspecting dupe who is inevitably left holding the (empty) bag! (For a discussion of the snipe hunt, see Smith 1957; and for its French analog, see Chartois 1945.)

The noise-making component of the snipe hunt reminds us of Lévi-Strauss's remark about the function of the same element in marriage charivari. He claims that "the function of noise is to draw attention to an anomaly in the unfolding of a syntagmatic sequence" (1969:288). It is the *breaking* of the syntagmatic sequence, according to Lévi-Strauss (1969:288), which is marked by the din produced by the wedding-party merrymakers. However, Lévi-Strauss tends to regard charivari as occurring primarily when the two principals being married are of unequal age, status, or wealth. Thus people marrying for a second or third time, or marrying someone much younger/older than themselves would very likely be subjected to a charivari (Lévi-Strauss 1969:286–87). Nevertheless, wedding customs elsewhere suggest that *all* newly-weds in Western cultures may be hazed and teased by some form of charivari (cf. Morrison 1974, and some of the other abundant charivari scholarship: Cocchiari 1949, 1950; Dömötör 1958; Alford 1959; Thompson 1972; Le Goff and Schmitt 1981; Rey-Flaud 1985). Lévi-Strauss's insight about the connection of noise-making with a sharp break in the continuity of daily life remains apt and I believe may be usefully applied to pranks in general.

We have already noted that pranks are commonly associated with individuals placed in some sort of *new* status or situation. This new status typically involves a break with the past. Accordingly, I contend that pranks are not only associated with rites of passage, but that pranks are so commonly markers of changes of status (joining a new group, e.g., a work force, attaining a new status, e.g., being married). Pranks in the United States are sometimes played upon a person on his or her birthday or when that person gets some kind of promotion or new job. All these contexts would qualify as changes of status.

Arnold van Gennep in his classic study *The Rites of Passage* which first appeared in 1908 observed that all rites of passage appeared to follow the same structural pattern: separation, transition, and incorporation to the society in question. Whether one speaks of puberty initiation rites, wedding rituals, or mortuary customs, the same sequence may be empirically observed. The individual is first separated from the group; then follows a marginal state in which the individual is temporarily neither fish nor fowl; and finally the individual is re-admitted back into society with his or her new status fully accepted (1960:vii). We can see this pattern exemplified when an individual travels from one country to another. First he formally exits from his country (showing his passport). Then for a time, he is neither in his own country nor yet admitted officially into the country to be visited (cf. transit lounges in international airports when one is physically in a given country but one has not been "officially" admitted into that country by going through customs and passport control of the country). This second stage of transition is surely a marginal one (cf. the marginal buffer zones often existing between borders of countries). Finally, the traveller reaches his destination and is formally admitted into that country.

Although Van Gennep does not discuss pranks per se, I would argue that his brilliant analysis of rites of passage does apply to this folklore genre. First the dupe is separated from the group by being sent on a wild goose chase. During the time he is on the false errand, he is in a marginal state. He is on the one hand part of the group, but on the other hand, he is not part of the group which often functions as a committee of the whole to prolong the time dimension of the prank. Different members of the group may encourage the dupe to continue on with the search for the nonexistent quest object. Finally, either the dupe comes to realize that he has been fooled or the joke is revealed to the victim by one or more members of the group. At this point, the victim is reincorporated into the group, e.g., as a full-fledged member in good standing.

If I am correct in seeing Van Gennep's famous rite of passage structural sequence in pranks, we can better understand why pranks are so appropriate for rites of passage themselves. The structure-in-miniature in pranks simply serves to mark the larger rite of passage being observed. One undergoes a rite of passage when one is married, and the successful completion of that rite is followed by a particular form of prank, namely, the charivari. The completion of the prank marks the end of the larger rite of passage; the newlyweds are now properly married and may be considered as normal members of the society at large once again.

How does this analysis of pranks help explain why pranks are played on the first of April? To understand this, we must remember that there are critical points in calendrical cycles. Such critical points may and indeed often are accompanied by rites of passage. Van Gennep himself recognized this—though without specific mention of April fool. "Those rites which accompany and bring about the change of the year, the season, or the month, should also be included in ceremonies of passage" (1960:178).

The months of March and April (and specifically the spring equinox) should be considered as the beginning of the year. In the northern temperate zones, it makes metaphorical sense for the year to begin with spring rather than on January 1st in the *dead* of winter. Historically, we know that the year did in fact begin with spring. The name of the twelfth month of December actually derives from the Latin word for ten. In the same way, November is nine, October is eight, and September is seven. Counting backwards, we can easily see that the year once began with March, not January. (In Iran to this day, March is considered the beginning of the new Iranian year.) Now we can understand that the month of April which comes a few days after the spring equinox marks the *new* year. April as a name comes from the Latin word meaning to "open" (cf. Cortsen 1937; Janssens 1958:119). Hence April, spring-time, the end of winter, the time for planting, is or at least was conceived of as the proper beginning of the year.

In this context, the first day of April is the opening day of a month whose name originally meant open. It is a critical day in the calendar insofar as April 1st may be construed as the end of the long period of death or dormancy, winter, and the beginning of a period of new life, spring. In the light of van Gennep's remark quoted above, April 1st marks a congruence of all his examples: a change of year, of season, and of month. April 1st is a calendrical rite of passage and accordingly it is appropriate to have pranks mark that date. Moreover, if fish are at all phallic, it would be equally reasonable to celebrate the welcome return to fertility by attaching paper fish to the clothing of April Fish victims.

Another linguistic piece of evidence supporting the interpretation proposed comes from the English custom of calling April first April Fools' Day or All Fools' Day. The latter designation cannot help but call to mind 'All Saints' Day' which is, of course, Halloween, All Hallows Eve which is celebrated on the evening of October 31st, that is, on the eve of November 1, All Saints' Day. In the United States, pranks are traditionally played on Halloween. Indeed, the only two calendrical dates which are specifically marked by pranks in the United States are April 1st and Halloween night. One could conceivably argue that Halloween provides a critical time shift. As April marks the end of winter and the beginning of spring, so Halloween marks the end of autumn (harvest) and the beginning of winter. The calendrical transitions from death to life (April Fools' Day) and from life to death (All Souls' Day) are both highlighted by the playing of pranks. It seems unlikely to me that the occurrence of pranks on these two particular dates is only a matter of coincidence.

If a prank is a microcosmic rite of passage, then we can for the first time appreciate why pranks should be played on the occasion of important rites of passage in both life cycles of individuals (birthdays, marriage) and the calendrical rites of passage for the community at large. Finally we can see that the association of pranks with the first of April is logically and psychologically appropriate.

We may again recall Lévi-Strauss's suggestion that the noise of charivari marked an intrusion in the normal syntagmatic sequence of everyday life. Generalizing from his one example, we may say that April 1st represents such an intrusive break. It is a ritual reversal of seasons. Winter to spring is such a reversal just as autumn to winter is a reversal. This disjunction in the flow of time is analogous to the unmarried becoming married, or a youth becoming an adult.

The reversal may be reflected in the reversal of power on April 1st as children play tricks on teachers and parents (or older siblings). Fiction understood as fact, falsehood as truth, is another instance of reversal. Pranks entail such features. On Halloween, boys may dress as girls; girls as boys; children as adults; and adults as children. The living may dress as the dead. (In the European origin of Halloween, the dead may return, posing as the living.) These reversals are part of the same pattern; they are temporary, not permanent. Boys who dress as girls on Halloween will revert to boys' clothes the next day. It is a limited time of ritual reversal. For a brief moment, individuals may be magically removed from their normal life (and gender) before being once again reintegrated into the routine of daily life. The reversal of time, of seasons, on April 1st is appropriately marked by a reversal from wisdom to April foolishness. Perhaps we do now have an answer to the question posed by the folk rhyme:

The first of April some do say,
Is set apart for All Fools' Day;
But why the people call it so,
Nor I, nor they themselves, do know.

REFERENCES CITED

Alford, Violet. 1959. Rough Music. *Folklore* 70:505–18.

Basile, Antonio. 1950. Il pesce d'aprile in Tripolitania. *Folklore* (Napoli) 5:113–14.

Baughman, Ernest W. 1966. *Type and Motif-Index of the Folktales of England and North America*. The Hague: Mouton.

Chartois, Jo. 1945. Hunting the Dahut: A French Folk Custom. *Journal of American Folklore* 58:21–24.

Christiansen, Reidar Th. 1947. Å narra april. *Syn og Segn* 53:126–34.

Cocchiara, Guiseppe. 1949/1950. Processo alle mattinate. *Lares* 15:31–41; 16:150–157.

Corso, Raffaele. 1920. Il pesce d'aprile. *Tutto*, II, no. 14 (4 aprile):58–59.

Cortsen, S.P. 1937. Der Monatsname Aprilis. *Glotta* 26:270–75.

Dömötör, Tekla. 1958. Erscheinungsformen des Charivari im Ungarischen Sprachgebiet. *Acta Ethnographica* 6:73–89.

Eichler, Lillian. 1924. *The Customs of Mankind*. Garden City: Garden City Publishing Company.

Gennep, Arnold van. 1960. *The Rites of Passage*. London: Routledge & Kegan Paul.

Grimm, Jacob and Wilhelm Grimm. 1854. *Deutsches Wörterbuch*. Erster Band A-Biermolke. Leipzig: Verlag von S. Hirzel.

Gubernatis, Angelo de. 1872. *Zoological Mythology*. Vol. I. London: Trübner & Co.

Honeyman, A.M. 1958/1959. Fools' Errands for Dundee Apprentices. *Folklore* 69/70:334–36.

Janssens, Prosper. 1958. Een-April, verzenderkensdag; betekenis en oorsprong. *Oostvlaamsche Zanten* 33:107–22.

Jungbauer, Gustav. 1927. April. In E. Hoffmann-Krayer and Hanns Bächtold-Stäubli, eds. *Handwörterbuch des Deutschen Aberglaubens*, Band I. Berlin und Leipzig: Walter de Gruyter. Pp. 555–67.

Laliberté, Monique. 1980. Le poisson d'Avril. *Culture & Tradition* 5:79–89.

Le Goff, Jacques and Jean-Claude Schmitt (eds.). 1981. *Le Charivari*. The Hague: Mouton.

Lemoine, Jules. 1889. Le poisson d'Avril en Belgique. *Revue des Traditions Populaires* 4:227–30.

Lévi-Strauss, Claude. 1969. *The Raw and the Cooked*. New York: Harper & Row.

Morrison, Monica. 1974. Wedding Night Pranks in Western New Brunswick. *Southern Folklore Quarterly* 38:285–97.

Müller, Joseph. 1923/24. Rheinische Aprilscherze und Neckrufe. *Zeitschrift des Vereins für Rheinische und Westfalische Volkskunde* 20/21:18–21.

Opie, Iona, and Peter Opie. 1959. *The Lore and Language of Schoolchildren*. Oxford: Clarendon Press.

Penick, Anne. 1954. Look Out, Newcomer! *Midwest Folklore* 4:239–43.

Pitrè, Giuseppe. 1902. *Curiosità di Usi Popolari*. Catania: Cav. Niccolò Giannotta.

Posen, I. Sheldon. 1974. Pranks and Practical Jokes at Children's Summer Camps. *Southern Folklore Quarterly* 38:299–309.

Rey-Flaud, Henri. 1958. *Le Charivari: Les rituels fondamentaux de la sexualité*. Paris: Payot.

Reynolds, Osborne M, Jr. 1984. Tortious Battery: Is 'I Didn't Mean Any Harm' Relevant? *Oklahoma Law Review* 37:717–31.

Rosières, Raoul. 1892. L'origine du Poisson d'Avril. *Revue des Traditions Populaires* 7:193–99.

Sébillot, Paul. 1888. Le poisson d'Avril. *Revue des Traditions Populaires* 3:184–88.

———. 1892. L'origine du poisson d'Avril. *Revue des Traditions Populaires* 7:309–10.

Smith, Johana H. 1957. In the Bag: A Study of Snipe Hunting. *Western Folklore* 16:107–10.

Tallman, Richard S. 1974. A Generic Approach to the Practical Joke. *Southern Folklore Quarterly* 38:259–74.

Thompson, E.P. 1972. 'Rough Music': Le Charivari Anglais. *Annales: Economies, sociétés, civilisations* 27:285–315.

Wight, John. 1927. April Fools' Day and Its Humours. *Word-Lore* 2:37–40.

Wolf-Beranek, Hertha. 1968. Zum Aprilscherz in den Sudetenländern. *Zeitschrift für Volkskunde* 64:223–27.

The Psychoanalytic Study
of the Grimms' Tales:
"The Maiden Without Hands" (AT 706)

Psychoanalysis began in the German-speaking world. Accordingly, it was inevitable that Freud and other early psychoanalysts interested in the content of folktales would turn to the major, principal corpus of tales in German, namely, the celebrated *Kinder- und Hausmärchen* of the brothers Grimm. Near the end of the first decade of the twentieth century, what has proven to be an incredibly large spate of analyses of individual Grimm tales by psychoanalysts began. One has only to consult such psychoanalytic bibliographical aids as Grinstein's multivolume *Index of Psychoanalytic Writings* (1950ff), the *Chicago Psychoanalytic Literature Index* (1920ff) or N. Kiell, *Psychoanalysis, Psychology, and Literature: A Bibliography*, 2nd ed. 2 vols. (1982) to discover essays by Maeder, Storfer, Silberer, Riklin, Abraham, Rank, Róheim, Bettelheim, and, of course, Freud himself.[1]

Freud in his 1913 paper "The Occurrence in Dreams of Material from Fairy Tales" understood that fairy tales could influence children's mental life and that these tales might be responsible for some of the content of patient's dreams. In the second of two case histories discussed, Freud interpreted both "Little Red Riding Hood" (AT 333) and "The Wolf and the Seven Little Goats" (AT 123).[2] Freud, incidentally, recognized that these two tales had "much in common with each other" and it is likely that modern folklorists would argue that the two are indeed cognate tale types. In this discussion, as well as in the first case history which involved a version of Rumpelstiltskin (AT 500), Freud more or less assumed the plot of these standard tales to be that of the Grimm version. This is even more explicit in another 1913 paper of Freud, namely "The Theme of the Three Caskets."[3] In this instance, Freud mentions no patients, but instead is concerned with analyzing the content of the folkloristic motif that Shakespeare borrowed for a scene in *The Merchant of Venice* (cf. Motif H511.1, Three Caskets, and AT 890, A Pound of Flesh). In the course of his argument, Freud remarks, "I will single out at this point the ninth of Grimm's Fairy Tales, the one with the title "The Twelve Brothers." He also makes reference to "The Six Swans" and to "another of Grimm's Tales 'The Goose-girl at the Fountain.'"

It is thus not difficult to document that when Freud wished to discuss fairy tale content, he invariably turned to the Grimm canon for his texts. And in similar fashion, his followers did likewise—with the notable exception of Géza Róheim who, having had early training in folkloristics, knew the importance of examining more than one version of a particular tale type under investigation.

Freud's primary interest in folktales was a therapeutic one; that is, by analyzing a patient's favorite tale or a tale that appeared in a patient's dreams, Freud hoped to discover something significant about the sources of that patient's mental problems. However, Freud also had a healthy intellectual interest in fairy tales per se. In his words, "If we carefully observe from clear instances the way in which dreamers use fairy tales and the point at which they bring them in, we may perhaps also succeed in picking up hints which will help in interpreting the remaining obscurities in the fairy tales themselves."[4] In sum, the psychoanalytic study of folklore could help with the treatment of individual patients, *and* the clinical study of patients e.g., including their free associations to dream symbols, might illuminate the latent content of fairy tales. The relationship between folklore and psychoanalysis was therefore understood to be mutually beneficial. Folklore could be of genuine assistance in the practice of psychoanalysis and psychoanalysis could be of possible value in elucidating the content of folklore.

One of Freud's most important contributions to folkloristics, *Dreams in Folklore*, a paper co-authored with classicist D. E. Oppenheim, was written circa 1911. Unfortunately, this paper was lost for many decades and did not actually appear in print until 1958. In this remarkable essay, Freud and Oppenheim selected folktales in which dreams occurred as part of the plot. In these tales, the dreams were typically interpreted either directly by one or more of the dramatic personae or by the dénouement of the story line. To Freud's astonishment and no doubt delight, the symbolic interpretation within the tale corresponded exactly with so-called Freudian exegesis of symbols. The fact that the symbolism employed in folktale dreams coincided with the psychoanalytic interpretations of the same symbols does not automatically prove the validity of such symbolic readings—both Freud and the folk might be in error. Still, the congruence of folk and analytic symbolic equations is an empirical fact which must be taken into account by those hostile to the psychoanalytic study of folklore.

In "The Ring of Fidelity," a tale found in Poggio's *Facetiae* chosen by Freud and Oppenheim, a man jealous of his wife had a dream in which a demon appeared. The demon promised him a foolproof way of ensuring his wife's remaining faithful. "Take this ring," instructed the demon, "and wear it on your finger with care. As long as you wear it, your wife cannot lie with any other man without your knowledge."[5] As the man awoke, excited with joy, he felt that he was pushing his finger into the vulva of his wife. Here in this tale, we find an explicit interpretation of the symbolism of finger rings, a symbolic meaning which remains current in contemporary wedding ritual wherein the groom pushes a ring on the outstretched finger of his bride. In this common conclusion of the wedding ceremony, the two participants signal their union by inserting a finger through a ring. The fact that the man holds the "female" ring and the woman extends a finger suggests that marriage allows the man and woman to manipulate each other's genitals.

It cannot be stressed strongly enough how valuable the explicit symbolic equations articulated in folklore texts are for the serious study of symbolism. No doubt skeptics upon hearing that the finger-ring ritual component of modern wedding ceremonialism has a phallic element will shake their heads in profound disbelief. Is there any hard evidence to support such an assertion? (Why do you suppose, incidentally, that the only good evidence is labelled "hard" rather than "soft"?) Consider for just a moment a tale contained in the Russian A. N. Afanasyev's mid-nineteenth century collection of bawdy folktales, published separately from the main corpus of Russian fairytales. The tale, entitled "The Enchanted Ring" tells of three brothers who seek marriage. The youngest mentions in public that, unlike his rich elder brothers, he is poor and that his only asset is "a tool that comes down to his knees." A merchant's daughter hears the remark and asks a marriage agent to arrange her marriage to the young man. "When the wedding night came, the bride found that her husband's tool was not as long as a finger." He explains to his outraged and disappointed bride that the expenses of the wedding forced him to pawn his masculine organ and that he needs fifty roubles to redeem it. The bride obtains the necessary funds from her mother and gives them to the young man. He sets off and meets a donor figure, an old woman, to whom he explains his difficulties. She offers to help and in exchange for the fifty roubles, she gives him a ring. "Take this ring, and put it only on your nail." The lad obeyed, and the same instant his prickle became a foot long. "Well," said the old woman, "is that long enough?" "But grannie, it is still not down to my knee." "You have but to put the ring lower, my son." He slipped the ring down to the middle of his finger, and immediately he had a "yard five miles long." The tale continues with the ring being stolen, and the thief who is riding in a carriage slips the ring down to the middle of his finger which results in his having an erection which "knocked the coachman off his box, passed over the horses and extended five miles in front of the carriage." The great Sicilian folklorist Giuseppe Pitré who provided the comparative notes for these tales of Afanasyev cites French and Norwegian parallels to the tale.[6] The critical theoretical point is that there is a direct association between placing a ring on a finger and phallic tumescence. Please note that the tale was collected before Freud was even born. It is precisely this kind of unequivocal, incontrovertible data which makes folklore so important for the study of symbolism. One need not be a Freudian at all to understand the symbolism of the ring in the Poggio or Afanasyev tales.

The tales used as a data base by Freud and Oppenheim did not come from the Grimms. Rather they came largely from traditional German tales contained in the pages of *Anthropophyteia* (1904–1913), a journal founded by folklorist F. S. Krauss in Vienna. This journal was designed to publish obscene folklore of the kind normally omitted from the standard collections made by nineteenth-century folklorists. This and the comparable French equivalent *Kryptadia* (1883–1911) from which Freud and Oppenheim also drew some texts did help to fill in the gap left by prudish folklorists unable or unwilling to oppose the strictures of censorship imposed by publishers—then and now. Freud not only wrote a letter of support for *Anthropophyteia*, at Krauss's request, but his name appeared as a member of the editorial committee for this periodical for volumes 7–9 (1910–1912), which further attests to his sincere interest in the study of folklore.

While it would be unfair to criticize the Grimm brothers for totally omitting all bawdy or obscene tales from their famous collection, the fact remains that censorship did play an important role in that collection. Anyone who has carried out folklore fieldwork knows very well that some informants do know traditional tales and songs with sexual content. Nothing of that sort appears in the hallowed Grimm canon. Given the nationalistic and romantic Zeitgeist of the Grimms' era, one can certainly understand why such tales did not appear, especially in a collection nominally directed at children. Nevertheless, to the extent that tales containing explicit sexual content do not appear in the Grimm tales, the collection simply cannot be regarded as totally representative of German folktales at the beginning of the nineteenth century.

It is sad to report that the battle against prudery and censorship in folkloristics is not yet over. In the Aarne-Thompson tale type index, the Grimm tales and essentially all Indo-European tales are assigned numbers followed by plot synopses. This is so except in the case of bawdy tales. We are told only AT 1420G *Anser Venalis. (Goose as Gift)*. The lover regains his gift by a ruse (obscene). The ruse remains unexplained. Or AT 1425, Putting the Devil into Hell. Obscene trick used to seduce woman. We are told nothing in this synopsis about the details of the obscene trick. Other examples include AT 1110* Hans Shows the Devil how Men are Made (Obscene) and AT 1728* The Parson and his Wife Naked in the Woods. (Obscene). The tale type index user is left to guess just how men are made or what happened to the parson and his wife.

The worst examples are tale types 1355*, 1356*, 1470*, 1546*, 1549*, and 1580*. Here we are told only "Obscene," which tells absolutely nothing about the contents of the tales so indexed. (Most are Livonian texts).

When the American folklorist Vance Randolph published his fascinating fairy tales from the Ozarks in the 1950s, again no bawdy examples were included. It was only in 1976 that the omitted texts, some of them at least, could appear in *Pissing in the Snow and Other Ozark Folktales.*[7] Whether it was Columbia University Press, the publisher of *We Always Lie to Strangers: Tall Tales from the Ozarks* (1951); *Who Blowed Up the Church House?* (1952); *The Devil's Pretty Daughter* (1955); *The Talking Turtle* (1957); and *Sticks in the Knapsack* (1958), who insisted that obscene texts be left out or whether it was self-censorship on Randolph's part, the results were the same. I mention this only to put into context the failure of the Grimms to include bawdy tales in their collection. If, in the late twentieth century, it is rare to find obscene tales published by scholarly journals and university presses, one cannot very well condemn the Grimm brothers for failing to include such tales in their collection.

In any event, with the exception of the tales analyzed in *Dreams in Folklore* by Freud and Oppenheim, nearly every single one of the dozens upon dozens of essays written on fairy tales by psychoanalysts makes use of the Grimm corpus. In this respect, psychoanalysts, like so many scholars in German literature and children's literature commit what is from the folklorist's perspective an unpardonable error of methodology. It has long been known that the Grimms, especially Wilhelm who was most concerned with the tales, re-wrote and doctored the tales they presented to the public. Despite the fact that the Grimms severely criticized Achim von Arnim and Clemens Brentano for adapting and modifying the folksongs contained in *Des Knaben Wunderhorn* (1805–1808) and that they early in their careers clearly called for the scientific collection of authentic folktales as they were orally told by peasants, the evidence reveals that the Grimm brothers failed to practice what they preached. They proved unable to resist succumbing to the temptation of combining elements from different versions of the same tale (type). The resultant *composite* texts were in fact never actually related by any one informant, although individual motifs or portions of a particular conflated text might have been. Folklorists refer to such composite texts as *fakelore* rather than folklore.[8] Fakelore does not include literature based upon or derived from folklore, e.g., those of Chaucer's *Canterbury Tales* which have close analogues among bona fide oral folktales. Fakelore refers to materials that are either fabricated totally out of whole cloth or are drastically altered and often bowdlerized rewritings of oral folklore *but yet are claimed to be pure oral tradition*. So while the first edition of the Grimm tales proclaimed that "No particular has been either added through our own poetic recreation, or improved and altered," the second edition of 1819 admitted "We have given many tales as one insofar as they complemented each other and no inconsistencies had to be excised in order to unite them; but if they diverged from each other, in which case each usually had its own characteristic features, we preferred the better of the tales, and kept the others for the notes."[9] The critical issue revolves around the statement "We have given many tales as one." Composite tales are fakelore, not folklore, though to the Grimms' credit, they at least admitted what they were doing.

The Grimm brothers are important for folkloristics for what they initially said they did, rather than for what they did. The goal of collecting oral folktales in the vernacular, and leaving them unaltered, was a laudable one—and this is so even if the Grimms were unable to live up to their own ideals. The sad point, from the folklorist's perspective, is that generations of Germanists have continued to limit their analyses of folktales to the Grimm canon. In the wake of the intellectual movement in large measure started by the Grimm brothers (or perhaps Herder), a host of folktale collections were undertaken around the world. These collections, especially in northern Europe, led Finnish folklorist Antti Aarne, at his mentor Kaarle Krohn's urging, to devise and publish a tale type index in 1910. This index, twice revised by American folklorist Stith Thompson in 1928 and again in 1961 has made it possible to locate many, many versions of a particular folktale in a matter of moments. So although folklorists are able to locate as many as one thousand separate versions of a given tale type, most of these printed and archival materials remain unnoticed and unused by non-folklorists.

Anyone who writes about Indo-European fairy tales without reference to the Aarne-Thompson (AT) classification system is almost certainly an amateur or dilettante from the folklorist's point of view. If a literary critic or psychoanalyst refers only to the Grimm version without indicating any awareness of that tale's AT number, one can be pretty certain that the writer is totally ignorant of the previous scholarship devoted to that tale as well.

From this vantage point, it should be easy to understand why folklorists cannot accept the methodology of psychoanalysts and others relying upon a *single* version of an international tale type as the sole basis of analysis and interpretation. Why, if there are one thousand versions of a folktale available for investigation, would anyone seriously interested in that tale choose to rely upon just one version of the tale, the Grimm version, keeping in mind that the Grimm version is *not* an authentic transcription from oral tradition. It is largely a literary, re-written composite text. If one wished to analyze nineteenth-century German culture on the basis of folktales, one would need to consult proper oral tales, not the Grimm versions. It is this sloppy and unscholarly inattention to source material which so infuriates folklorists when they attend conferences devoted to the Grimm tales or when they read the countless essays devoted to tale types whose authors insist upon referring only to the Grimm texts.

Folktales, like other genres of folklore, are originally an oral creation, existing in oral performance. Any written version is only a pale shadow or reflection of the oral artform of the storyteller. The Grimms, imbued as they were with heartfelt sentiments of incipient nationalism and romanticism, did not give us anything like the best, that is, most faithful to the oral tradition, versions of the tales they elicited. What this means essentially is that one must decide whether one is concerned with (1) the true folktales, or (2) the Grimms' particular re-writes of those tales. One can certainly study the Grimm brothers and the various editions of the tales they reported, but unless one goes back to their original field notes, one is *not* dealing with pure oral tradition. Anyone studying

Grimm tales should not be deluded into thinking they are examining authentic fairy tales.

Consequently, when we read the various psychoanalytic treatments of the Grimm tales, we must remember the limitations inherent in restricting the analysis to Grimm texts only. Having considered the factor of source criticism, we must nevertheless indicate that many of the psychoanalytic studies of Grimm tales are not without insight. To the extent that folktales, especially fairy tales (Aarne-Thompson tale types 300–749), the so-called magic tales, deal with fantasy rather than reality, they do require psychological interpretation. Mainstream folklorists have tended to be literal, not symbolic in orientation, preferring historical, not psychological treatments. Thus anti-psychological folklorists seek to find *actual* customs and practices referred to in the Grimm tales, rather than realizing that fairy tales represent fiction, not fact. Of course, one could argue that some psychoanalysts, like literal-minded folklorists, also try to find fact underlying fiction. For example, in a highly speculative but provocative note in 1923, Karl Abraham, one of the first and most brilliant of Freud's early group, suggested that the sequence of events in "Tischchen deck dich, Goldesel und Knuppel aus dem Sack" (KHM 36, AT 563, The Table, the Ass, and the Stick) corresponded to the supposed three stages of infantile reality: oral, anal, and genital. In terms of wishful thinking, the hero obtains first a magic table or table-cloth which provides an infinite amount of food, clearly an oral magic object. Next, the hero obtains a gold-dropping ass which would represent the anal phase of development. And finally, the hero is given a stick that beats an enemy until called off. Through this phallic stick, the hero defeats the wicked innkeeper/father figure. In Abraham's words, "The fairy-tale thus contains three wish-fulfilments corresponding to the three erotogenic zones. It is noteworthy that their sequence coincides with the three phases of libido development discovered by Freud."[10]

It is hard to convey just how adamantly opposed to psychoanalytic interpretation the majority of conventional scholars are. The anti-psychological bias is so strong among folklorists that they don't even mention the numerous psychoanalytic essays devoted to Grimm tales in print. To cite just one illustrative example out of many, Géza Róheim, originally a Hungarian folklorist who upon exposure to psychoanalysis became perhaps the first psychoanalytic anthropologist, was a prolific writer and he analyzed a dozen or so Grimm tales in some depth. Róheim is rarely, if ever, cited by folklorists. For instance, Róheim undertook an analysis of the Grimm version of Aarne-Thompson tale type 480 in his essay "Dame Holle: Dream and Folk Tale (Grimm No. 24) published posthumously in 1953, the same year that Warren Roberts completed his doctoral dissertation on the tale type at Indiana University. In 1958, Roberts published his dissertation under the title of *The Tale of the Kind and the Unkind Girls*. Róheim's analysis is not cited. In 1982, Walter Scherf in his useful *Lexikon der Zaubermärchen* provided a brief survey of the scholarship devoted to this Grimm tale and many others. Róheim's analysis is not mentioned. Max Lüthi, perhaps the greatest living folktale scholar, in his exemplary *Märchen*, the seventh printing of which was published in 1979, makes no mention of any of Róheim's analyses in his section of the book specifically devoted to the psychological approach. For that matter, even Bruno Bettelheim in *The Uses of Enchantment*, first published in 1976, a book that is explicitly psychoanalytic in approach, fails to cite anything written by Róheim. Similarly, Carl-Heinz Mallet's *Kennen Sie Kinder?* (1981), a psychoanalytically informed analysis of four Grimm tales, fails to make any reference to Róheim. This is unfortunate inasmuch as Róheim had offered psychoanalytic readings of at least three of the tales: Hansel and Gretel (AT 327A), Little Red Riding Hood (AT 333) and the Boy Who Set Out to Learn Fear (AT 326) thirty years earlier.[11] To be sure, most psychoanalysts are not scholars and most of those who write on Grimm tales are unaware of previous studies made by other psychoanalysts.

The situation is roughly as follows: folklorists and psychoanalysts have for nearly a century analyzed the Grimm tales in almost total ignorance of one another. Folklorists blindly committed to anti-symbolic, anti-psychological readings of folktales make little or no effort to discover what, if anything, psychoanalysts have to say about the tales they are studying. Psychoanalysts, limited to their twentieth-century patients' free associations to the nineteenth-century Grimm versions of folktales, are blithely unaware of the existence of hundreds of versions of the same tale types so assiduously assembled by folklorists in archives or presented in painstaking detail in historic-geographic monographs.

It may be well nigh impossible to wean psychoanalysts away from the Grimm tales, classical mythology (especially the tale of Oedipus) and the Bible. After all, psychoanalysts have only a marginal interest in folklore. They have neither the time nor the intellectual curiosity to wade through technical monographs summarizing hundreds of versions of a given tale type. For this reason, it is probably more realistic to ask that folklore scholars and others genuinely concerned with folktales try to overcome their bias in order to consult what psychoanalysts have had to say about the tale they are investigating. If the psychoanalytic interpretation is farfetched or unsupported by empirical data, it may and indeed certainly should be rejected. But there is no excuse, in my view, for a scholar to refuse, *a priori*, to look at any interpretation of a tale under study. My experience is that colleagues and students alike simply reject Freudian interpretations out of hand. When asked what of Freud or his followers they have read on folklore, they usually reply that they have read little or nothing. They are simply opposed to Freudian theory on general principle. This is hardly an intellectually defensible position. Theories and interpretations should be accepted or rejected on the basis of some kind of critical examination. The closed mind is not one likely to advance the field of folkloristics.

One reason for the resistance of literal-minded folklorists to the psychoanalytic approach to folktales might have to do with a basic fear of discovering why they are so utterly fascinated by the content of such folktales. Folklorists, like so many academics, will go to any lengths to deny that folktales (or any folklore for that matter) refer to basic human drives and emotions. Assembling large numbers of versions, mapping them, plotting possible paths of diffusion, e.g., from India or the Middle East, or applying syntagmatic (Proppian) or paradigmatic (Lévi-Straussian) structural models to folktale plots all successfully avoid the necessity of facing up to the possibility of latent meanings. The longstanding effort to dehumanize folktales by reducing them to motifs, themes, or tale type summaries, or dots on a map, or a series of binary oppositions (centering on the distinction between nature and culture) has been an all too consistent hallmark of folkloristics for more than a century. Yet these same folklorists who *reduce* fairy tales to tale types and motif numbers complain that Freudian theory is reductionistic! Reductionism, of course, is neither good nor evil. No one criticizes Einstein's formula $E = MC^2$ for being reductionistic. If reductionism adds to our understanding of the world around us, it may be worthwhile. If reductionism consists of a mechanistic reading of a narrative which does not illuminate our appreciation of its content, it should be rejected.

The possibility that folktales might represent artistic projections of sibling rivalry and inter-generational conflict, e.g., son-father, daughter-mother, has evidently been beyond the realm of the credible for the majority of professional folklorists. We know from Propp's 1928 *Morphology of the Folktale* that at least in Russian fairy tales, the syntagmatic sequence begins with the dissolution of a nuclear family—Function 1: One of the members of a family is absent from home—and ends with the formation of a new one—Function 31: The hero is married and ascends the throne. Propp's analysis was based upon a corpus of some one hundred tales from the Afanasyev collection of Russian fairy tales. Are we justified in assuming that Propp's scheme applies to German fairy tales and to the Grimm tales in particular? To the extent that the Afanasyev Russian fairy tales are international tale types (with Aarne-Thompson numbers), it is perfectly legitimate to expect that Propp's analysis would indeed apply to the general tale types in each instance and that would include the Grimm tales.

Granting that assumption, we can extrapolate from the Proppian formula of thirty-one possible functions that fairy tales are concerned with heroes and heroines breaking away from initial nuclear family structures in order to get married, that is, to form new nuclear families.[13] Regarding Propp's pioneering formulation as a fanciful and fantastic *cursus honorum* for adolescent boys and girls, we are in a far better position to appreciate the potential of psychoanalytic insights into the nature of family inter-personal dynamics. Fairy tales, though not really intended solely for an audience exclusively made up of children, are always told from the child's point of view, never the parents'. The Grimms' labeling of their collection as *Kinder- und Hausmärchen* actually was a disservice to the field of folklore insofar as the original tales were told around hearths for *all* members of the family, not just the children. In times before writing, printing, and the modern media of radio, television, and motion pictures, oral tale-telling was standard evening entertainment fare. However, although the tales were equally enjoyed by adult members of the audience, the fact remains that it is invariably children who are the protagonists of the fairy tales. One must keep in mind that a person never ceases to be the child of his or her parents. Even an elderly grandparent remains in some sense in his or her own private mind a child vis-à-vis his or her own parents. Fairy tales, viewed from a psychoanalytic perspective, represent a classic arena for the playing out of time-honored interpersonal conflicts.

If Propp's formula is valid, then the major task in fairy tales is to replace one's original family through marriage. Thus a girl must break away from her mother and father to find a prince with whom to live happily ever after, and a boy must break away from his father and mother to find a princess to do likewise. Thanks to Propp's delineation of the standard dramatis personae in fairy tales, we can understand why a boy may split his father imago into two elements, a kind male donor figure who aids the hero, and a mean male antagonist (dragon, giant) who seeks to impede the hero. In similar fashion a girl may encounter a good mother or surrogate figure (helpful cow, fairy godmother) in order to defeat a wicked (step) mother (witch, ogress, etc.) It is true that the sex of the donor figure may vary. Sometimes a good mother figure may help the boy while a kindly old man may help the girl. But the same-sex opposition between protagonist and antagonist does remain pretty consistent in fairy tales.

The advantages of the psychoanalytic approach are obvious in understanding the nature of giants and giantesses. To be sure, the literal-minded folklorists are convinced that there must have been once a race of giant people who dwelled on earth. According to such reasoning, the giants in fairy tales are then survivals of historical fact. There is no physical anthropological evidence to support such an interpretation. What is much more likely is that we have in fairy tales a projection of the infant's eye view of parents. Parents, to the infant's eye, are huge versions of the infant. They have the same basic features as the infant but on a gigantesque scale. From the "infantocentric" perspective, the baby does not see itself as being small. Rather the parents appear to be large. One of the basic premises of psychoanalytic theory is that infant is to parent as hero or heroine in fairy tales is to supernatural entities. (In religion, the formula would be: infant or child is to parent as adult is to god or goddess.) In this light, every single individual has had the experience of encountering "giants" who are nothing more than caricatures of parents writ large.

If fairy tales are projections of children's maturation, then we can better appreciate the symbolic means of expression of that process. Whether a princess has to learn to get used to having a frog in bed with her (and to force herself to kiss it so that it may take human form) (Grimm #1, AT 440) or whether Gretel manages to force the witch to enter her own oven, a superb and totally feminine triumph over the wicked mother figure in Hansel and Gretel (Grimm #15, AT 327A), the basic story-line is the same. One must not be deceived by the title Hansel and Gretel. It is definitely Gretel's story, not Hansel's. It is the struggle of a girl against a would-be food-providing nurturant mother figure. The eating of the witch's gingerbread house is an act of oral aggression against the body of the evil mother. The final act of having the witch burn up in her own oven (sexual cavity) is the ultimate repudiation of the mother figure.[12]

Let us reconsider Frau Holle (Grimm 24, AT 480) in this context. What have the folklorists told us about the meaning of this well-known fairy tale? Warren Roberts, after laboriously amassing approximately one thousand versions of this tale, concludes that the original form of the tale "probably originated in the Near East at some time before 1400 and passed to Northern Europe by way of the area between the Black and Caspian Seas."[13] Roberts makes no attempt to discuss the possible meaning or meanings of the tale. In this respect, he is unfortunately all too representative of practitioners of the historic-geographic or Finnish method.

Actually, earlier scholars had proposed interpretations of the tale. Nature mythology advocates argued that the heroine was the aurora, and the pearls which dropped from the heroine's mouth in the Perrault version were the dew. In a competing reading, myth ritualists claimed the heroine was the Spring, loaded with bountiful gifts while the bad girl was the Winter.[14] A 1923 German dissertation by Hans Hempel contended that Frau Holle in the Grimm version is a vegetation demon of the kind defined by Mannhardt. The Hungarian folklorist Janos Honti argued in contrast that the message of the tale "in its widest implication is that a good and modest girl is rewarded and a haughty one is punished."[15]

Frau Holle and its cognates which fall under the rubric of Aarne-Thompson tale type 480 is not a story about the dawn and the dew or the purported anthropomorphic struggle between spring and winter. Such interpretations succeed only in diverting the reader away from the latent content of the tale. Solar mythologists used to boast that one great advantage of their methodology was that it explained (away) the apparently disgusting and irrational elements in myth. From a psychoanalytic point of view, such theories are themselves a form of projection insofar as earthly and earthy acts are projected onto far-away heavenly *bodies*!

Róheim treats the tale as a dream in which the persecuted daughter falls into the dream-well. He interprets the tasks as symbolic weaning: apples from a tree or a calf taken from a cow. Taking the loaf out of the oven, Róheim suggests, is the heroine's pulling her younger sister out of her mother's womb. His oral reading of the tale is supported by his observation that the awakening sequence reflects the same bias, the girl has roses or pearls fall from her mouth.[16] However, Róheim presents no evidence in support of his interpretation—as is so typical of psychoanalytic readings of Grimm tales. It is argument by assertion. The reader is presumably expected to accept on faith the *ex cathedra* pronouncements of the psychoanalyst.

In critiquing Róheim's interpretation of Frau Holle, I believe that it is not necessary to accept his dream origin of the tale. Tales may or may not stem from dreams. It is just as logical to assume that dreams derive from fairy tales. An individual dreams and the dreams could well be influenced by the content of tales heard by that individual. One must not be fooled by the fact that if one can remember dreams well enough to relate them the next morning, one invariably puts them in narrative form. So regardless of what the actual structure of the dream may have been, it is usually "told" as a narrative and so thereby resembles other forms of narrative including fairy tales. In any event, it is always risky to assume that any one mental creation is necessarily the origin of others. Why not imagine instead that *both* dreams and fairy tales reflect the unconscious wishes and thoughts of individuals in a given culture? Dream and fairy tale are thus in tandem, bearing similar structure and content perhaps, but neither one being necessarily the source of the other.

Those scholars who detected a similarity or parallelism in fairy tales and initiation rites may have been on the right track. One can see a pattern in girls' puberty rites that is reminiscent of fairy tales in which girls are the protagonists. The mistake of Winterstein in his 1928 essay "Die Pubertätsriten der Mädchen und ihre Spuren im Marchen" and of Vladimir Propp in his 1946 *Historical Roots of the Wondertale* is analogous to Róheim's error in assuming a dream origin of fairy tales. The fact that there might be a parallel between the maturation sequence of girls' fairy tales and actual initiation rituals does not require that the rituals are the historical source of the fairy tales. Once again we find the anti-symbolic, pro-literal bias at work. Fantasy derives from fact as psychology is turned into history. We need not believe that straw was ever spun into gold or that asses ever defecated gold. But without some form of psychological theory, such fantastic motifs are destined to continue to frustrate the literal-historical minded folklorists.

In Frau Holle and other female-centered fairy tales in the Indo-European tradition, a girl confronts her emerging femininity which includes her gender's sexual characteristics. Some of the specific traits in the tale type bear this out. In several versions, a girl kills her mother at the suggestion of a widow.[17] Here we have wishful thinking on the part of a young girl who follows orders to kill her mother. In terms of the Electra complex, she kills the rival mother figure, but since she follows someone else's orders, she is more or less free from guilt.

In a great many versions, the action of the tale begins at or near a well. The symbolism of wells is fairly obvious. The standard

motif *Kinderbrunnen* (Motif T589.6.4 Children said to come from
a well) indicates the female genital nature of this symbol. Consider
some of the motifs cited by Roberts: "The heroine spins until her
fingers are bloody and must wash the blood from the spinning apparatus."[18] If spinning is masturbatory, then the initial rupturing
of the hymen can produce blood. In some versions, the heroine
climbs down the well in pursuit of a lost spindle.[19] It should be
stressed that the symbolism involved is not limited to any one tale.
The sudden bleeding of a heroine is to be found in other fairy
tales. In Fitchers Vogel (Grimm 46, AT 311), we have an example
of the "forbidden chamber." In such tales, a young woman is permitted to go anywhere in a house except into one room. She vio-
lates the interdiction and an egg and/or key becomes bloody. She
is unable to wash the bloodstain out and is thus caught by the vil-
lain. It would be hard to imagine that the literal folklorists would
be able to locate a historical basis for motif C913, Bloody key as
sign of disobedience. But from a psychoanalytic viewpoint, the
forbidden chamber is clearly the vaginal area and the bloody key
is a symbol of the loss of chastity. Perhaps not unrelated is the
detail that the erring maiden typically finds other young women
beheaded in the chamber. One is tempted to speculate that these
earlier victims are merely young girls who have lost their *maiden
heads*. In any event, bloody keys do not occur in reality, but only
in fantasy.

To return to Frau Holle, we may interpret the specific tasks in
the light of physiological maturation. As a young girl matures, her
breasts develop. Apples are a standard symbol for breasts. So
"Apple tree is shaken or apples picked" might represent this phase
of pubertal development. "The cow is milked," another task,
might suggest the final stage of physical maturation. After a young
woman gives birth, milk magically appears in her breasts and she
must accustom herself to giving milk—as a cow gives milk to a calf.
"An oven filled with bread asks to have the bread removed"[20] reflects the same event. An oven is a standard womb symbol—one
thinks of the Anglo-American folktale of Jack and the Beanstalk
(AT 328) in which the giant's wife helps Jack—against her own
husband—by hiding the boy in her oven.[21] So removing the bread
could be construed as an invitation to bear children. The linkage

between these tasks, symbolically speaking, is entirely logical. Bread removed from an oven (bearing children), picking apples (ripe, mature breasts) and milking a cow (nursing an infant) are all events which follow the onset of menstruation or losing one's chastity.

The reward in Frau Holle and cognate tales is typically something valuable which falls from her mouth. In this example of displacement upwards, the body aperture is clean and beautiful. This is consonant with the tasks in many versions of the tale where the young initiate is especially concerned with keeping a hut or house (= body) clean. The "dirty" aspects of one's emerging sexuality (including blood) have been transformed so that either she spits pearls or she chooses a box or coffer which contains valuables. The unkind girl does not know how to respond to the challenges of emerging physiological maturity and so she spits ugly things from her mouth or selects a container with reptiles, frogs, or toads. The vagina as mouth is signalled not only by the existence of the vagina dentata motif (F547.1.1) but also by the term "labia" which literally means lips.[22] If a vagina is a mouth, a mouth can be a vagina. This is why it makes perfect sense, psychoanalytically speaking, for the successful heroine to have nice things fall from her "mouth" at the end of the tale.

From this interpretation of AT 480, we may now appreciate some of the more puzzling aspects of the tale type. For example, in the Following the River Subtype (as opposed to the Encounters Enroute Subtype), "The heroine is sent to wash animal intestines and the river carries them off." One might speculate that this is a task concerned with cleansing an internal body part, intestines. Washing intestines is thus a wish to cleanse a body part, an impulse related to the reaction against the culturally sanctioned notion that one's body contains dirt. Washing animal intestines could be understood as a vain effort to cleanse oneself of one's dirty animalistic properties.

Another curious subtype identified by Roberts as "The Strawberries in the Snow" requires the heroine to gather strawberries in midwinter. This form of AT 480 would seemingly offer support for the summer-winter ritual calendrical interpretation of the tale. But equally likely is the reference to fruition and fertility. A girl's ability to find flowers or ripened fruit in the middle of winter could once again be a metaphor for the quest for human fertility. The unkind girl is typically frozen in this form of the tale. This too would seem to be an appropriate metaphor for frigidity or the lack of fertility.

The puzzling motifs of individual versions of tale type 480 and analogous heroine-centered fairy tales can, thanks to psychoanalytic insights, be seen in a new light. For example, in a striking Sicilian version of AT 425, The Search for the Lost Husband, the heroine's tasks include having to praise as beautiful "a stream of blood" and a "door which opens and closes by itself."[23] From a logical perspective, these tasks seem odd indeed; from a *psycho*logical perspective, they make perfect sense. And it is more precisely the psychoanalytic approach which allows the interpreter of folklore to make sense of apparent non-sense! The flow of blood which must be praised could be the onset of menses. Anything which acts by itself or plays by itself can be a convenient symbol for masturbatory behavior. In this case, the fact that it is a "door" which opens and closes by itself supports this interpretation.

By combining Propp's *Morphology* and the psychoanalytic approach, we can now better understand why AT 480 is so frequently combined with other tale types, e.g., AT 403, The Black and the White Bride, and AT 510A, Cinderella. From Propp's analysis we know that fairy tales normally end with marriage. Since AT 480 does not, we can readily appreciate why it functions as an introduction to these other tale types which do end with marriage. From a psychoanalytic vantage point, we can understand why a young girl has to come to terms with her budding physiological maturation (in symbolic terms) before entering into marriage. We might remark that an insightful analysis of a Dogon version of AT 480 by Calame-Griaule demonstrates how the initiation elements of such maturation have been translated into appropriate symbols for an African context. She notes, "The initiatory voyage in our tale . . . does not so much make reference to real rites (even though certain elements are recognizable) as refer to that quest for fecundity that characterizes the Dogon woman from infancy."[24] Calame-Griaule rightly remarks that her analysis of a version of AT 480 in Africa could illuminate versions of the tale told in Europe, calling particular attention to the heroine's bloodied distaff in the Grimms' "Frau Holle" as a sign of the girl's puberty.

It is clearly not possible to offer psychoanalytic readings of every tale in the Grimm canon within the confines of a single paper. Such a project would require a book-length tome and a fairly substantial one at that. For the present purposes, it ought to be sufficient simply to indicate what such an approach can yield in the way of increased understanding and appreciation of the tales collected by the Grimm brothers. As already noted, there is considerable literature devoted to the psychoanalytic exegeses of the Grimm tales which literary scholars and folklorists are obviously free to consult should they have the slightest interest in so doing.

I should like to conclude my plea for the psychoanalytic study of the Grimm tales by examining briefly one additional tale, namely, "Das Mädchen ohne Hände" (Grimm 31, AT 706, The Maiden Without Hands). In the Grimm version of this standard Indo-European tale type, a poor miller is promised wealth by an old man if he will give the old man what stands behind his mill. The miller accepts, thinking that what stands behind his mill is his apple tree. He then returns home to discover that it was his daughter who had been standing behind the mill at that moment. (Please note the symbolic equivalence of apple trees and daughters in this tale. The daughter was obviously the apple of the miller's eye!) When the devil (old man) comes to claim his prize, the girl has washed herself clean and has drawn a chalk circle around her. The devil, frustrated, demands that the miller cut off the girl's hands. Reluctantly the miller does so. The girl wanders off into the forest, and meets a king who has silver hands made for her. After marriage, the king is deceived by the devil too when a message indicating that his queen has given birth is altered to say she bore a monster. The king's letter in return is likewise changed by the devil to instruct the court to put the queen and her child to death. She flees with her child. The king returns and goes in search of her. An angel aids him and eventually he, his queen, and their child are reunited.

From the tale type summary, we learn that the father's sale of his daughter to the devil is just *one* rationale for why the heroine has her hands cut off. Much more common is the fact that the heroine refuses to marry her own father. Often it is she who cuts her own hands off in response to the advances made by her father (cf. motif T411.1, Lecherous father). Incidentally, this is why it would be methodologically disastrous to rely solely upon the Grimm version of this tale type for analysis. The lecherous father motif is only hinted at and the heavy Christian overlay involving devils and angels is also uncharacteristic.

How are we to understand the central salient motif of this tale: the cutting off of the heroine's hands? Does this reflect an actual custom? If so, what evidence is there for the existence of such a custom? With the innovations in plastic surgery and the creation of ingenious prostheses in modern times, the miraculous restoration of the missing hands could now be understood as historically plausible. But at the beginning of the nineteenth century when the Grimms collected this tale, it was not. The tale goes back at least to the thirteenth century when such a medical miracle was even less likely.

There is another crucial question about the tale. Why, if it is the *father* who was making improper advances (= selling his own daughter/apple tree to the devil in return for wealth), should it be the daughter who is punished? In the normal morality of the fairy tale universe, it is villains who are punished, not innocents.

The abundant scholarship devoted to Aarne-Thompson tale type 706 is typical enough. There have been one hundred years of dissertations, monographs and articles devoted to the "Maiden without Hands." Highlights include Russian folklorist Alexander N. Veselofsky (1837–1906) whose edition of *Novella della figlia del re di Dacia* was published in Pisa in 1866. Hermann Suchier's seventy-page introduction in 1884 to *Oeuvres poetiques de Philippe de Remi, Sire de Beaumanoir* offered perhaps the first major survey of the many literary and folktale versions of the plot (cf. Suchier, "La Fille sans mains," *Romania* 30 (1901): 519–538). Also in 1884 appeared an important essay by Th. de Puymaigre, "La Fille aux mains coupées," *Revue d'histoire des Religions* 10 (1884): 193–209.

In 1893, Marian Roalfe Cox published *Cinderella* based upon some 345 versions, a truly remarkable achievement in assembling comparative materials in the pre-tale type index era. As one of her subtypes, "Catskin" which we now know as AT 510B, The Dress of Gold, of Silver, and of Stars (Cap o' Rushes), began with such motifs as "Death-bed promise," "Deceased wife's resemblance" or "Deceased wife's ring marriage test" or "Deceased wife's shoe marriage test" and "Unnatural father," she included an extended discussion of "The Maiden without Hands" in her preface. As a matter of fact, more than twenty of her seventy pages of preface are devoted to this tale even though technically it is not considered part of the Cinderella cycle. One of her 345 texts, a Serbian tale (# 169) is actually a version of AT 706 and not of 510B, but one cannot fault Cox inasmuch as she was working at a time when tale typology was in its infancy. It remains a theoretical possibility that AT 706 and AT 510B are closely related subtypes of the same basic tale type which includes Cinderella AT 510A and Love Like Salt (AT 923), the ultimate source for Shakespeare's *King Lear*.[25]

The list of scholarly treatments of the tale continues. A. B. Gough in 1902 published *The Constance Saga*, which discussed the tale following the earlier research of Suchier. In 1905, the Serbian scholar Pavle Popović published a monograph on the tale: *Prepovetka o devojci bez ruku* (Belgrade, 1905). See also Pavle Popović, "Die Manekine in der südslavischen Literatur," *Zeitschrift für Romanische Philologie* 32 (1908): 312–322. Other treatments include Josef Klapper, "Das Märchen von dem Mädchen ohne Hände als Predigtexempel," *Mitteilungen der Schlesischen Gesellschaft für Volkskunde* 10 (1908): 29–45; Rodolfo Lenz, "Un grupo de consejas chilenas," *Anales de la Universidad* [Chile] 129 (1911): 685–764, 1339–1393; 130 (1912): 209–214, 369–377 (see esp. "La niña sin manos," pp. 715–733, 1352–1370); and Heinrich Däumling's inaugural-dissertation *Studie über den Typus des 'Mädchens ohne Hände' innerhalb des Konstanze-Zyklus* (München, 1912). (It is fascinating that a man whose name means thumbling should write a monograph about a maiden who lost her hand!) An excellent survey of folktale versions including Slavic texts appeared in Svetislav Stefanović, "Ein Beitrag zur Angelsächsischen Offa-Sage" *Anglia* 35 (1911–1912): 483–525. Then, of course, there is the usual thorough coverage of versions in Johannes Bolte and

Georg Polívka, *Anmerkungen zu den Kinder- und Hausmärchen der Brüder Grimm*, vol. 1 (Leipzig, 1913), pp. 295–311.

Margaret Schlauch in her Columbia University doctoral dissertation, first published in 1927 under the title *Chaucer's Constance and Accused Queens*, discussed the tale type en passant (e.g., pp. 35–39, 64–77). J. N. Lincoln, "The Legend of the Handless Maiden," *Hispanic Review* 4 (1936): 277–280 synopsized twenty Hispanic versions of the tale. The following year folklorist Alexander Haggerty Krappe discussed the tale in his essay "The Offa-Constance Legend," *Anglia* 61 (1937): 361–369, the same year that John Warren Knedler, Jr., filed his 464-page Harvard doctoral dissertation " 'The Girl without Hands: A Comparative Study in Folklore and Romance.'" This historic-geographic study of AT 706 was based upon 183 texts. Knedler later published "The Girl Without Hands: Latin-American Variants," *Hispanic Review* 10 (1942): 314–324.

The impressive array of monographs and articles may be concluded with mention of Vytautas Bagdanavičius, *Cultural Wellsprings of Folktales* (New York, 1970), pp. 101–148; Hélène Bernier, *La Fille aux mains coupées (conte-type 706), Les Archives de Folklore* 12 (Quebec, 1971) who analyzes 33 French-Canadian and French-American versions, 48 French versions, and 96 Irish versions of the tale; Suzanne Ruelland, *La Fille sans mains (Analyse de dix-neuf versions africaines du conte type 706)* (Paris, 1973); and Corneliu Bǎrbulescu, "The Maiden Without Hands: AT 706 in Romanian Folklore," in Linda Dégh, ed., *Studies in East European Folk Narrative* (Bloomington, 1978), pp. 319–365. This presentation of twenty-four versions had been previously published in Romanian in the *Revista de Etnografie si Folclor* in 1966.

These various studies thoroughly document the tale's popularity in both oral and literary tradition. The literary tradition of the story includes versions in the Offa legend from the middle of the thirteenth century, the *Manekine*, dating from 1270 in the works of Philippe de Remi (1246–1296) and the French romance of "La Belle Hélène de Constantinople" from the late thirteenth century.[26] There can be no question of the tale's continuous popularity for at least seven centuries. What have folklorists had to say about the meaning of this curious tale? Stith Thompson observes "Few collections of any extent in all of Europe from Ireland to eastern Russia fail to have this story" and "The oral tale is so popular and so widely distributed that it deserves more study than it has yet received."[27]

Yet it has received considerable study at the hands of folklorists. What kinds of conclusions have they reached? Knedler in his study of eleven Latin-American versions is able to show by comparative motif analysis that at least seven of these did not come from Spain but from France, probably Brittany. His conclusion is that although one might logically think that the Latin American versions came from Spain, the comparative method can prove otherwise. From this scholar who wrote his doctoral dissertation on the tale we get no interpretation of the father-daughter incest motif and no plausible explanation of why the heroine's hands should be cut off.

Perhaps no interpretation is preferable to the nature-mythological theories in vogue in the nineteenth century. Veselovsky in his edition of *Novella della Figlia del Re di Dacia* (Pisa, 1866) claimed the plot came from an earlier myth: So the queen who dies is the goddess of the departing summer; her daughter, the goddess of the coming year; the father is the god Wotan; the hunter who discovers the fugitive is winter; the cut-off hands are the falling leaves. The hands are restored after being touched by life-bringing water just as leaves and grass come back to life through spring rains.[28] Through such an interpretation, the unpleasant or disgusting details of the apparent father-daughter incest theme are happily avoided or explained away.

In speaking of the father-daughter incest theme which occurs at the beginning of Catskin, Henry Charles Coote in 1880 advocated the "sun and dawn theories of Cox, De Gubernatis and Max Müller." Coote observed, "Without the application of this or some other esoteric view the story is certainly revolting and perhaps inexplicable."[29] Coote continues, according to such a theory, the heroine is to be understood as Aurora, the dawn, who is a young, beautiful goddess, daughter of the old sun. "This young Aurora the old sun, her father, pursues, and wishes to wed, for the former Aurora, her mother, has died and left him alone. The father anticipates that the new dawn will equal in beauty the one which is gone."[30] Similarly, Svetislav Stefanovič, after discussing more than a dozen versions of AT 706, concludes that the circle of tales with the theme of a daughter pursued by a lecherous father goes back to a very old, certainly general Indo-European myth of the following of the dawn (Aurora) by her father the sky-god.[31] The slight variation of the sky-god rather than the sun doesn't alter the basic nature-mythological interpretation.

Folklorist Krappe's comment on the tale is that the episode of "the attempted incest is so monstrous to Occidental feeling . . . so revolting, in such contradiction with West European thought" that the tale could not have originated in Europe. Instead, he contends, it must have arisen in the Byzantine East where one finds other stories of marriage among persons of near kin.[32] This reminds us of one of the most ingenious attempts to rationalize the incest motif, namely, the theory proposed by Margaret Schlauch. Using the nineteenth-century evolutionary theory which assumed that matriarchy (and matrilineal descent) was everywhere prior to patriarchy, Schlauch, following a suggestion made by Frazer with respect to several fables recorded by Hyginus that contained instances of father-daughter incest, hypothesized that a king living in a matriarchal system had power only through his wife, the queen. If and when she died, he became powerless. The queen-mother's sovereignty would pass to her daughter and that daughter's husband would thus assume the place formerly occupied by the king. According to Frazer's reasoning, the king was bound to vacate the throne on the death of his wife, the queen, since he occupied it only by virtue of his marriage with her. Hence if the king desired to reign after his wife's death, the only way in which he could legitimately continue to do so was by marrying his daughter, and so prolong through her the title which had formerly been his through her mother.[33] Although Frazer had made his remarks without reference to tale type 706, Schlauch felt that his explanation might be applicable to fairy tales. This type of rationalization clearly falls into the historical-literalist category since it assumes that father-daughter incest actually occurred.

If Krappe and other folklorists had been the slightest bit willing to consider psychoanalytic theory seriously, they might possibly have realized that it is precisely because the attempted incest is so monstrous to Occidental feeling that it occurs in fairy tale form. Krappe's undisguised hostility to the psychoanalytic approach is easy to document. In perhaps his best-known work, *The Science of Folklore* (1930), he refers to what he terms the "hallucinations of the psychoanalytic school of Vienna. . . . The very premises put forward by that school, the existence of various 'complexes,' operative in their view, during infancy and childhood, being unproven, the deductions therefore would be quite untenable even if their logic were faultless. As a matter of fact, it is anything but that."[34] He continues his tirade in a footnote: "For the entertainment of the reader I quote Karl Abraham, *Dreams and Myths*. . . . The monograph is a translation from the German. Evidently there is always money enough available for the rendering into English of trash of this type. . . ."[35] Krappe was not alone. Archer Taylor in his 1940 survey "Some Trends and Problems in Studies of the Folk-Tale" took only one sentence to dismiss the approach. "The endeavors to solve the mystery of folk-tales by the even more puzzling mysteries of psychoanalysis can now be laid on the shelf to gather dust."[36] This would appear to be a fine example of wishful thinking!

Let us look at the tale itself. The Romanian oral versions are certainly representative. One begins: "An emperor who was left a widower, unable to find a woman more beautiful than his daughter, resolved to make her his wife." The girl tries to flee but "her father got wind of her intentions and cut off her hands from the wrist."[37] This is the essence of the tale type. What is the logic, if any, which underlies these strange and in Krappe's terms "monstrous" events?

Several other Romanian versions may be cited. In one, we learn the following details: "On her deathbed, an empress told her husband, the emperor, that if he married again, he should take for his wife only the woman whose foot fitted into her shoe. After long years of searching, the daughter, who had meanwhile grown up, chanced to put the shoe on. On discovering that, the emperor decided to marry her." The girl flees but later the father finds her in the forest where he "cuts off her hands and nose and left her to her fate."[38] In yet another Romanian version, "A landowner's wife on her deathbed told her husband not to marry again unless he found the girl whose finger would fit her ring. Since the ring fitted no finger except his daughter's, the landowner decided to marry her."[39] In this version also, the heroine's hands are cut off. The alternation of what Cox labelled the "Deceased wife's ring marriage test" and the "Deceased wife's shoes marriage test" is traditional as her comparisons of Catskin texts attest.

One of the principles from psychoanalytic theory that might be of use in explicating this tale type is projective inversion. "I hate you" becomes through projective inversion "You hate me." This allows an individual to project his feelings to the object of those feelings. By this device, the individual is freed from guilt. It is not that I hate you, but rather that you hate me. In sociological parlance, this has been termed "blaming the victim." Otto Rank in his pioneering *The Myth of the Birth of the Hero* (1909) gave an excellent example of projective inversion (although he did not call it that). He pointed out that in the standard Indo-European hero biography, the hero's father tries to kill the hero at birth. But Rank observed that Indo-European fathers wanted sons. It was rather a case of sons who wanted to kill their fathers (for Oedipal reasons), and this could not be admitted. Hence in the story-lines, it is invariably fathers who attempt to kill their sons, which thereby frees these sons from any feelings of guilt. When the sons kill their fathers, it is strictly a matter of self-defense.

The early psychoanalysts were not so insightful in analyzing female-centered folklore, although to be sure, Riklin in his monograph *Wunscherfüllung und Symbolik im Märchen* (1908) did comment in his discussion of tales in which fathers attempted to marry their own daughters that the initial death of the mother (queen) reflected wishful thinking on the part of adolescent girls who, in terms of the Electral complex, wanted to replace their mothers vis-à-vis their fathers. There can be no guilt for the girls inasmuch as the mother presumably dies of natural causes. The father is instructed to find someone as beautiful as the mother or someone who can fit into the mother's shoe or ring. The sexual symbolism of shoes is well documented and survives in such modern folklore as the custom of placing shoes on the rear bumpers of cars carrying newlyweds off to their honeymoons or in the most well-known version of Cinderella, or in such nursery rhymes in which old women who live in shoes have lots of children. The similar symbolism of finger-rings was discussed earlier in this paper.

The alternation of the shoe and the ring test for marriage with the father is a fine illustration of what has been termed the symbolic equivalence of allomotifs. According to this empirical methodology for investigating the symbolism of folktales (and other folkloristic genres), the contents of a given motifemic slot (or Propp's function) are evidently regarded as equivalent by the folk insofar as the story line is advanced in the same fashion no matter which allomotif is employed.[40]

There is abundant independent evidence supporting the female genital symbolism of both shoes and rings. Both are placed upon external appendages such as feet and fingers and can serve as metaphorical microcosms for heterosexual coitus. One thinks of the custom cited by Ernest Jones of throwing an old slipper or shoe after the departing newlywed couple with the explicit accompanying saying "May you fit her as well as my foot fits this old shoe."[41] With respect to the association of shoes and marriage, it is clear that the "glass" slipper which occurs in several versions of the tale of Cinderella (AT 510A) is an appropriate symbol for virginity. Glass is fragile and once broken cannot be repaired. The defloration imagery is also expressed in a wedding ritual which entails a literalization of the pertinent metaphor. The bride immediately after the ceremony rises above the crowd to throw away her bridal bouquet thus indicating her assent or readiness to be deflowered.

The oft-cited but totally specious theory that the "glass" of Cinderella's slipper was a mistranslation of the French word "vair" (fur) which somehow became "verre" (glass) is but one more instance of the literal-minded folklorist's refusal to read fairy tales symbolically. Since there are no such things as glass slippers, literalists had a problem. From their perspective, glass must have been a "mistake." Slippers are made of fur, not glass. Hence the ingenious vair-verre proposal. But the motif in question is glass, not fur, slippers and the motif occurs in versions of the tale in languages other than French where the homonymic wordplay doesn't work. Folklorists have been trying for at least a century, in vain, to point out the absurdity of this "fur" interpretation of the glass slipper. What is most fascinating about this misinterpretation is that "fur" carries much of the actual underlying symbolic import of the glass slipper—a reference to the pubic hair surrounding the female genital area. This suggests that *interpretations* of fairy tales and their appeal may reflect the same unconscious message as the very tales they purportedly claim to explicate.[42]

Fairy tales represent the child's point of view. The maiden without hands is a girl who wants to marry her father, but this taboo cannot be expressed directly. So through projective inversion, it is the father who wants to marry his daughter. This is not to say that there may not be fathers who are sexually attracted to their own daughters, but only that in fairy tales, it is the daughter's point of view which is articulated. In carrying out the dead mother's commands, the father is obliged to marry his own daughter. Since, according to this interpretation, it is the girl who is guilty of the original incestuous thought, it is appropriate that it is the girl who is punished for this thought. This is why it is the girl who is punished by having her hands cut off. Schlauch reminds us that "Sometimes the hands are cut off as punishment for her stubbornness in resisting her father; sometimes as in *La Manekine*, their loss is a voluntary act of self-mutilation."[43] In the latter case, it is the girl herself who cuts off her own hands. In some of the literary versions of the plot, the king admires his daughter's hands so she therefore persuades her servant to cut them off or she cuts off one hand. She then sends her hands to her father in a silver dish covered with a cloth.[44] This version of AT 706 is quite similar to AT 706B, Present to the Lover, in which a maiden sends to her lecherous brother or lover her eyes or hands or breasts that he has admired.[45]

But the vexing and perplexing question remains: why the hands? Actually, there have been theories proposed, but they are hardly convincing. Knedler in his 1937 doctoral dissertation takes a predictable literal-minded approach. He devotes a chapter to a classical Greek ritual called "Maschalismos" in which murderers allegedly cut off the extremities of their victims. It is not explained why Greek murderers so mutilated the corpses. Knedler suggests that the "amputation in the Girl Without Hands cycle should be viewed against the background of . . . the rite of *maschalismos*."[46] There is no evidence whatsoever to support such a hypothesis. Nor would it explain why the hands in particular are cut off—as opposed to other body extremities.

In 1982, a curious psychoanalytic reading of Beaumanoir's *La Manekine*, a *circa* the year 1270 literary version of AT 706, proposed an equally unlikely explanation of the hand-cutting episode. According to this view, castration anxiety is the key. The heroine's "hand becomes a phallus, distributed, transferable—both her father's and her own." Then "because her severed hand is to be interpreted as representing a phallus, she must be considered not just a woman, but a phallic woman."[47] Again, I see little evidence to support such an interpretation.

Why the hands? Possibly because the father has asked for his daughter's *hand* in marriage. The idiom exists in German too: "um die Hand anhalten (werben)." This kind of punning play on words is common enough in both dreams and fairy tales. Since the father is after his daughter's hand, he takes it literally. Another possibility is that it is the hands of an adolescent girl which might be guilty of masturbatory behavior—just like the heroine of AT 480 playing with a spindle near a well. If the actions of hands initiated the masturbatory fantasy on the part of a young girl with respect to replacing her mother and marrying her father, then the sinning hands could be punished under the rubric of *lex talionis* which requires that the punishment fit the crime. Otto Rank in his classic *Das Inzest-Motiv in Dichtung und Sage* (Leipzig: Franz Deuticke, 1926), first published in 1912, offered such an interpretation in his brief discussion of the tale. He understood the cut-off hand as self-inflicted punishment for masturbatory activity, which itself substitutes for sexual involvement with the father.[48]

There is some textual evidence which can be adduced in support of the sexual sinning of hands. For example, a legend attached to Pope Leo among others reports that as he was celebrating Easter mass, a woman kissed his hand. This aroused him sexually and shortly thereafter he withdrew to cut off the hand which had scandalized him. Later, the people complained because he did not celebrate mass as usual. He prayed to the Virgin who appeared to him and restored the missing hand.[49] Incidentally, this might help explain why the faithful insist upon touching or kissing the foot of the statue of Saint Peter in St. Peter's in Rome. It brings the same good luck as that of a rabbit's "foot" often attached to a male's keyring.

A touching scene also occurs in a literary version of AT 706, namely, the *Figlia del re di Dacia* wherein the heroine cuts off her hand on the Virgin's orders because her father has thrust her hand into his bosom "and into a more dishonorable place."[50] Remembering such principles as wishful thinking and projective inversion, we can see why the heroine feels that her sinning hand should be cut off.

I don't expect any audience hostile to psychoanalytic theory to accept this reading of AT 706, but I would point out that at least it is an interpretation which offers some explanation of the "monstrous" events so repugnant to European thought. The tale type is about incest—that is overt and explicit. And the heroine's hands are cut off. That is part and parcel of the plot. Those skeptical of the invoking of the principle of projective inversion to explicate these critical details are invited to propose some alternative explanation. The fact that a half-dozen dissertations and full-fledged monographs have proposed no explanation whatsoever for the co-occurrence of the threat of father-daughter incest and the hand-cutting detail suggests that it is not so easy to do so. From the psychoanalytic perspective, the remainder of the tale also makes sense. Fleeing from her father's advances, the heroine, handless, nevertheless manages to marry royalty (a father substitute) after all, and bear a child. (The Electral fantasy often includes bearing the father's child and in that way totally replacing the rival-mother.)

The false accusation that the heroine has given birth to a monster is consonant with the interpretation advanced here. The "monstrous" crime of incest was thought in medieval times to lead to the birth of literal monsters.[51] Marriage leads to the restoration of the heroine's hand. In metaphorical terms, someone appropriate has asked for and received the heroine's hand in marriage. The message, so to speak, is that in society, a girl must resist the temptation or impulse to marry her father but must leave home to marry someone else. We come back again to Propp's basic formula for all Indo-European fairy tales—beginning with the dissolution of the initial nuclear family and the formation of a new one. To Propp, we need to add Freud in order to have a more comprehensive understanding of these fairy tales.

Those clinical psychologists and psychoanalysts who have probed the possible relationship between fairy tale content and adolescent maturation might well appreciate AT 706, The Maiden without Hands, and the above analysis. Those who have written on fairy tales in terms of their being a pre-scientific form of developmental psychology seeking to show how boys become men and girls become women could have cited AT 706 with profit.[52] At least some of the feminist critics of fairy tales have noticed the tale: "Time and again in fairy tales boys are sent off on adventures for seven years or so. What do girls do in similar circumstances? They are repressed; they must not speak or laugh; they must sit in a tree and dew or undergo some similar initiation into martyrdom. Girls have their hands cut off, are sent to live with monsters, all to save their father from death until their brothers or husband arrives back to inherit the kingdom. In short, they are taught to be passive victims."[53] I am not sure that the feminist critics have entirely understood the unconscious content of such tales as AT 706. Many female-centered fairy tales have the heroines delivering themselves from initial difficulties. A girl who succeeds in fantasy form in killing off her mother is hardly a passive victim of circumstance!

Regardless of whether or not the above interpretation of AT 706 is deemed valid, I hope that I have succeeded in demonstrating the possible utility of a psychoanalytic approach to fairy tales in general and the Grimm tales in particular. But even if I have done this, a dilemma remains. The academic prejudice against psychoanalytic theory persists. Folklorists who are surrounded by scores of versions of tales containing literally fantastic material remain adamant in their refusal to look at this rich data psychoanalytically. A folklorist writing an essay in 1984 "Evaluating Psychoanalytic Folklore: Are Freudians Ever Right?" notes how few folklorists make any use of psychoanalytic theory.[54] So the psychoanalytic study of folklore by default is left to psychoanalysts who are not scholars and who do not possess any special expertise in folkloristics. For most psychoanalysts, the analysis of Grimm tales is more or less a hobby or avocational pursuit. It allows them to publish papers—in various psychiatric journals. Some of these papers are insightful, but the vast majority are amateurish, inadequately researched essays tending to be rigid, dogmatic applications of Freudian theory to a single version of a tale type. This means that although psychoanalysts are willing to apply psychoanalytic theory to folklore, they do so in a closed universe. They limit their data base to the Grimm canon, classical mythology and the Old Testament. As a result, the psychoanalytic study of the Grimm tales which started with Freud himself is likely to remain in the hands of a few select psychoanalysts whose publications will not be read by mainstream professional folklorists.

I think the psychoanalytic approach to fairy tales is too important to be left in the hands of psychoanalysts. I believe the Grimm tales and more significantly the hundreds of undoctored oral cognates deserve better. They represent the most authentic and aesthetically beautiful creations of the Indo-European mind. But if they are fantasy, let them be analyzed as such. The literal-historical approach has its good points, but it cannot possibly plumb the depths of the fantastic. One of the most common types of traditional foolishness involves a simpleton understanding or rather misunderstanding a metaphor in literal terms (cf. Motifs J2450–J2499, Literal fools). To the extent that the Grimm tales and their cognates are based upon metaphor and symbol, the exclusively literal approach to these tales constitutes a kind of academic foolishness. So long as folklorists insist upon being numskulls, the field of folkloristics is likely to remain on the periphery rather than in its rightful place at the center of the general humanistic and social scientific inquiry investigating the very best products of human imagination.

NOTES

1. For a general overview, see Alan Dundes, "The Psychoanalytic Study of Folklore," *Annals of Scholarship* 3(3) (1985): 1–42. Representative discussions include Elizabeth Heimpel, "Märchen und Psychologie," *Sammlung* 8 (1953): 278–293; Gabrielle Leber, "Über tiefenpsychologische Aspekte von Märchenmotiven," *Praxis der Kinderpsychologie und*

Kingerpsychiatrie 4 (1955): 274–285; Emanuel K. Schwarts, "A Psychoanalytic Study of the Fairy Tale," *American Journal of Psychotherapy* 10 (1956): 740–762; Glauco Carloni, "La fiaba al lume della psicoanalisi," *Revista di Psicoanalisi* 9 (1963): 169–186; Hans E. Giehrl, *Volksmärchen und Tiefenpsychologie (München: Ehrenwirth Verlag, 1970),* and Charlotte Bühler and Josefine Bilz, *Das Märchen und die Phantasie des Kindes,* 4. Auflage (Berlin: Springer-Verlag, 1977), the latter being a revised edition of a work which first appeared in 1917.

2. Sigmund Freud, "The Occurrence in Dreams of Material from Fairy-Tales," in *Collected Papers,* vol. 4 (New York: Basic Books, 1959), 236–243.

3. Freud, "The Theme of the Three Caskets," in *Collected Papers,* vol. 4 (New York: Basic Books, 1959), 244–256.

4. Freud, "The Occurrence in Dreams of Material from Fairy-Tales," 239.

5. Sigmund Freud and D. E. Oppenheim, *Dreams in Folklore* (New York: International Universities Press, 1958), 61.

6. Aleksandr N. Afanasyev, *Russian Secret Tales: Bawdy Folktales of Old Russia* (New York: Brussel and Brussel, 1966) 65–76, 269–270. For a Norwegian version collected by Asbjørnsen, see Oddbjørg Høgset, ed., *Erotiske folkeeventyr* (Oslo: Universitetsforlaget, 1977), 58–61. Incidentally, the tale is in all probability a variant of AT 560, The Magic Ring, one of whose constituent motifs is D1662.1, Magic ring works by being stroked. This motif has masturbatory overtones as does motif D1662.2, Magic lamp works by being stroked, a central element in AT 561, Aladdin.

7. Vance Randolph, *Pissing in the Snow & Other Ozark Folktales* (Urbana: University of Illinois Press, 1976). This was only one of the six manuscript volumes of "unprintable" folklore collected by Randolph. One set of these volumes is to be found in the library of the Kinsey Institute for Sex Research at Indiana University. For an idea of the nature and scope of Vance Randolph's important contributions to American folklore, see Robert Cochran and Michael Luster, eds., *For Love and For Money: The Writings of Vance Randolph* (Batesville, Arkansas: Arkansas College Folklore Archive Publications, 1979).

8. The term "fakelore" was coined by Richard M. Dorson. See his "Folklore and Fake Lore," *American Mercury* 70 (1950): 335–343, and "Fakelore," *Zeitschrift für Volkskunde* 65 (1969): 56–64. For a discussion of the Grimm tale as fakelore, see Alan Dundes, "Nationalistic Inferiority Complexes and the Fabrication of Fakelore: A Reconsideration of Ossian, the *Kinder- und Hausmärchen, the Kalevala,* and Paul Bunyan," *Journal of Folklore Research* 22 (1985): 5–18, pp 40–56 this volume.

9. John M. Ellis, *One Fairy Story Too Many: The Brothers Grimm and Their Tales* (Chicago: University of Chicago Press, 1983), 13, 17.

10. Karl Abraham, "Two Contributions to the Study of Symbols," in *Clinical Papers and Essays on Psychoanalysis*, vol. 2 (New York: Basic Books, 1955), 81–85. For other psychoanalytic considerations of this tale type, see Roy Huss, "Grimms' 'The Table, the Ass and the Stick': A Drama of the Phallic Stage," *Psychoanalytic Review* 62 (1975): 167–171, and Mahmoud Omidsalar, "Oedipus in Kansas: A Version of Aarne-Thompson 569 (Grimm No. 54) among the Potawatomi Indians," *American Imago* 40 (1983): 159–174. For another attempt to find "the three stages of psychosexual development" in a single folktale, see Mohammad Shafii and Sharon Shafii, "Symbolic Expression of Developmental Conflicts in a Persian Fairy Tale," *International Review of Psycho-Analysis* 1 (1974): 219–225.

11. For Róheim's analysis of Hansel and Gretel, see his "Hansel and Gretel," *Bulletin of the Menninger Clinic* 17 (1953): 90–92. For his analyses of Little Red Riding Hood and Fearless John, see "Fairy Tale and Dream," *The Psychoanalytic Study of the Child* 8 (1953): 394–403. For other analyses of Grimm tales by Róheim, see "Psycho-Analysis and the Folk-Tale," *International Journal of Psycho-Analysis* 3 (1922): 180–186; "The Story of the Light That Disappeared," *Samiksa* 1 (1947): 51–85; "The Bear in the Haunted Mill," *American Imago* 5 (1948): 70–82; "The Wolf and the Seven Kids," *Psychoanalytic Quarterly* 22 (1953): 253–256; "Dame Holle: Dream and Folk Tale (Grimm No. 24)," in Robert Lindner, ed., *Explorations in Psychoanalysis* (New York: Julian Press, 1953), 84–94; and "The Language of Birds," *American Imago* 10 (1953): 3–14. Those who failed to cite Róheim's excessively Freudian but nonetheless fascinating exegeses of fairy tales include Warren E. Roberts, *The Tale of the Kind and the Unkind Girls: Aa-Th 480 and Related Tales* (Berlin: Walter De Gruyter, 1958); Walter Scherf, *Lexikon der Zaubermärchen* (Stuttgart: Alfred Kröner Verlag, 1982); Max Lüthi, *Märchen* (Stuttgart: Metzler, 1979); Bruno Bettelheim; *The Uses of Enchantment: The Meaning and Importance of Fairy Tales* (New York: Vintage, 1977); and Carl-Heinz Mallet, *Kennen Sie Kinder? Wie Kinder denken, handeln und fühlen, aufgezeigt an vier Grimmschen Märchen* (Hamburg: Hoffmann und Campe, 1980). The English edition is *Fairy Tales and Children* (New York: Schocken, 1984).

12. For evidence that the oven can be a symbol for the female pudendum, see Eric Partridge, *A Dictionary of Historical Slang* (Harmondsworth: Penguin, 1972), 655; and Ernest Borneman, *Sex im Volksmund: Der obszöne Wortschatz der Deutschen* (Reinbek bei Hamburg: Rowohlt, 1971). Borneman notes, for example, the idiom "Brot im Ofen" to refer to an unborn fetus. Freud discusses oven-womb symbolism in his "Symbolism in Dreams" lecture in *A General Introduction to Psychoanalysis* (Garden City: Permabooks, 1953), 170.

13. Warren E. Roberts, *The Tale of the Kind and the Unkind Girls*,163.

14. Roberts, p. 4, citing P. Saintyves, *Les Contes de Perrault et les récits parallèles* (Paris: Librairie Critique Émile Nourry, 1923), 9–11.

15. János Honti, "The Tale—Its World," in *Studies in Oral Epic Tradition* (Budapest: Akadémiai Kiadó, 1975), 33. The reference to Hans Hempel, *Das Frau Holle-Märchen und sein Typus* (Greifswald, 1923) is from Roberts, p. 5. For a similar moral interpretation of the tale, see Steven Swann Jones, "Structural and Thematic Applications of the Comparative Method: A Case Study of 'The Kind and Unkind Girls,'" *Journal of Folklore Research* 23 (1986): 158–159.

16. Géza Róheim, "Dame Holle: Dream and Folk Tale (Grimm No. 24)," in Robert Lindner, ed., *Explorations in Psychoanalysis: Essays in honor of Theodor Reik* (New York: Julian Press, 1953), 89.

17. Roberts, 79. This type of detail is not explained by the "initiation" approach. See A. Winterstein, "Die Pubertätsriten der Mädchen und ihre Spuren im Märchen," *Imago* 14 (1928): 199–274; or the selections from Vladimir Propp's 1946 *Historical Roots of the Wondertale* in Propp, *Theory and History of Folklore* (Minneapolis: University of Minnesota Press, 1984), 100–123.

18. Roberts, 79.

19. Roberts, 76.

20. Roberts, 84. For evidence of the apple-breast symbolism, see Borneman, *Sex im Volksmund* and Freud, *A General Introduction to Psycho-Analysis*, 163. Gail Ann Kligman in her M.A. in folklore thesis "A Socio-psychological Interpretation of 'The Tale of the Kind and Unkind Girl' " (University of California, Berkeley, 1973), p. 57 suggests that the various tasks all permit the expression of aggression against the heroine's mother's body, e.g., apples and cows referring to the maternal breasts.

21. For further consideration of the symbolism of this tale, see Alan Dundes, ed., *The Study of Folklore* (Englewood Cliffs: Prentice-Hall, 1965), 107–113.

22. Weston La Barre, *They Shall Take Up Serpents: Psychology of the Southern Snake-Handling Cult* (Minneapolis: University of Minnesota Press, 1962), 89n. I believe that one possible "origin" of the vagina dentata motif might stem from a transformation of the male's early aggressive impulses expressed through his teeth towards the maternal breast. Biting the breast is a standard means for an infant to indicate feelings of satiety or anger towards the mother. As male teeth initially threatened a projection from a female body, the breast, so later in life, teeth located in a vagina threaten a projection from the male body, the phallus. For references to vagina dentata legends, see Dundes, *The Study of Folklore*, 164, n. 18.

23. Laura Gonzenbach, *Sicilianische Märchen*, vol. 1 (Leipzig: Wilhelm Engelmann, 1870), 99. The interesting motifs were cited but not ex-

plained by Ralph Troger in his *A Comparative Study of A Bengal Folktale: Underworld Beliefs and Underworld Helpers: An Analysis of the Bengal Folktale Type: The Pursuit of Blowing Cotton—AT 480* (Calcutta: Indian Publications, 1966), 27.

24. Geneviéve Calame-Griaule, "The Father's Bowl: Analysis of a Dogon Version of AT 480," *Research in African Literatures* 15 (1984): 168–184. (The quotation is from p. 180.) For the original, longer essay, see "La Calebasse Brisée: Etude du Theme Initiatique dans Quelques Versions Africaines des 'Deux Filles' (T 480)," *Cahiers de Littérature Orale* 1 (1975): 23–66.

25. However, AT 706 is not included in the Cinderella tale complex by Anna Birgitta Rooth in her *The Cinderella Cycle* (Lund: C. W. K. Gleerup, 1951) nor by Max Lüthi in his "Der Aschenputtel-Zyklus," in *Vom Menschenbild im Märchen*, Veröffentlichungen der Europäischen Märchengesellschaft, Band 1 (Kassel: Im Erich Röth-Verlag, 1980) 39–58. For a discussion of AT 923, see Alan Dundes, " 'To Love My Father All': A Psychoanalytic Study of the Folktale Source of *King Lear*," *Southern Folklore Quarterly* 40 (1976): 353–366, reprinted in *Interpreting Folklore* (Bloomington: Indiana University Press, 1980), 211–222.

26. Knedler claims there are at least forty literary variants of the tale. See John Warren Knedler, Jr., "The Girl Without Hands: A Comparative Study in Folk-Lore and Romance," unpublished doctoral dissertation, Harvard University, 1937, 28. For surveys of the previous scholarship devoted to the tale, see Knedler, 251–284, or Walter Scherf, *Lexikon der Zaubermärchen* (Stuttgart: Alfred Kröner Verlag, 1982), 266–267. For additional discussions, see Lynn King Morris, *Chaucer Source and Analogue Criticism: A Cross-Referenced Guide* (New York: Garland, 1985), 137–140.

27. Stith Thompson, *The Folktale* (New York: The Dryden Press, 1951), 121.

28. Alessandro Wesselofsky, *Novella della figlia del re di Dacia* (Pisa: Nistri, 1866), xxxi–xxxii. For reactions, most critical, see Th. de Puymaigre, "La Fille Aux Mains Coupées," *Revue de l'Histoire des Religions* 10 (1884): 207; Marian Roalfe Cox, *Cinderella* (London: David Nutt, 1893), lxii, n.1; and John Warren Knedler, "The Girl Without Hands: A Comparative Study in Folk-Lore and Romance," 259. For references to other mythological interpretations of the tale, see Hermann Suchier, *Oeuvres Poétiques de Philippe de Remi, Sire de Beaumanoir* vol. 1 (Paris: Librairie de Firmin Didot, 1884), lxxix, and A. B. Gough, *The Constance Saga* (Berlin: Mayer & Müller, 1902), 2, n.2.

29. Henry Charles Coote, "Catskin: The English and Irish Peau D'Ane," *The Folklore Record* 3(1) (1880): 1–25. The quotation is on p. 20.

30. Coote, 21.

31. Svetislav Stefanovič, "Ein Beitrag zur Angelsächsischen Offa-Sage," *Anglia* 35 (1911–1912): 524.

32. Alexander Haggerty Krappe, "The Offa-Constance Legend," *Anglia* 61 (1937): 367.

33. Margaret Schlauch, *Chaucer's Constance and Accused Queens* (New York: Gordian Press, 1969), 40–41.

34. Alexander Haggerty Krappe, *The Science of Folklore* (New York: W. W. Norton, 1964), 14.

35. Krappe, 43, n. 31.

36. Archer Taylor, "Some Trends and Problems in Studies of the Folk-Tale," *Studies in Philology* 37 (1940): 17.

37. Corneliu Bărbulescu, "The Maiden Without Hands: AT 706 in Romanian Folklore," in Linda Dégh, ed., *Studies in East European Folk Narrative*, Indiana University Folklore Monograph Series 25 (Bloomington: Folklore Institute, 1978), 351.

38. Bărbulescu, 341.

39. Bărbulescu, 345.

40. For a discussion of this methodology, see Alan Dundes, "The Symbolic Equivalence of Allomotifs in the Rabbit-Herd (AT 570)," *Arv* 36 (1980)[1982]: 91–98.

41. Ernest Jones, "Psychoanalysis and Folklore," in Alan Dundes, ed., *The Study of Folklore* (Englewood Cliffs: Prentice-Hall, 1965) 96. For a sample of the abundant literature devoted to shoe symbolism, see G. Aigremont [Siegmar Schultze], *Fuss- und Schuh-Symbolik und Erotik* (Leipzig: Verlags-Aktien-Gesellschaft, 1909); Jacob Nacht, "The Symbolism of the Shoe with Special Reference to Jewish Sources," *Jewish Quarterly Review* 6 (1915): 1–22; William A. Rossi, *The Sex Life of the Foot and Shoe* (New York: Ballantine Books, 1976); and Dorothee Kleinmann, "Cendrillon et son pied," *Cahiers de Littérature Orale* 4 (1978): 56–88. See also Maureen Duffy, *The Erotic World of Faery* (London: Hodder and Stoughton, 1972) 270.

42. For a discussion of the fallacious vair-verre interpretation of Cinderella's glass slipper, see Paul Delarue, "From Perrault to Walt Disney: The Slipper of Cinderella," in Alan Dundes, ed., *Cinderella: A Folklore Casebook* (New York: Garland, 1982), 110–114.

43. Schlauch 71, n. 16. For other examples of voluntary mutilation, see A. B. Gough, *The Constance Saga, Palaestra* 23 (Berlin: Mayer & Müller, 1902): 17.

44. Gough, 24.

45. For discussions of this tale type, see Marjorie Williamson, "Les Yeux Arrachés," *Philological Quarterly* 11 (1932): 149–162, and Angel González Palencia, "La Doncella Que Se Saco Los Ojos," *Revista de la Biblioteca, Archivo Y Museo* 9 (1932): 181–200, 272–294. (This latter reference is incorrectly cited in the tale type index.)

46. Knedler, 319.

47. Thelma S. Fenster, "Beaumanoir's *La Manekine*: Kin D(r)ead: Incest, Doubling, and Death," *American Imago* 39 (1982): 41–58. The quotations are on pp. 50–51.

48. Rank, *Das Inzest-Motiv in Dichtung und Sage*, p. 366 and p. 361, n. 4, cited by Fenster, p. 52, n. 18. See also Sandor Ferenczi, "Embarrassed Hands," in *Further Contributions to the Theory and Technique of Psycho-Analysis* (London: Hogarth Press, 1926), 315–316. According to Ferenczi, often people who hide their hands under tables or in pockets are expressing insufficiently repressed tendencies towards onanism. Even the Jungians recognize that "the handlessness of the girl had to do with her father-complex" although there is no explicit reference to sexuality or masturbation. See Marie-Louise von Franz's discussion of the tale in her *Problems of the Feminine in Fairytales* (New York: Spring Publications, 1972) 70–94. (The quotation comes from p. 79.) For another Jungian reading of AT 706, see Hans Dieckmann, *Twice-Told Tales: The Psychological Use of Fairy Tales* (Wilmette, Illinois: Chiron Publications, 1986), 88–100.

49. This legend is cited by Puymaigre, pp. 208–209, and Knedler, p. 220. See also Frederic C. Tubach, *Index Exemplorum: A Handbook of Medieval Religious Tales*, FF Communications No. 204 (Helsinki: Akademia Scientiarum Fennica, 1969) 191, # 2419 Hand restored by Virgin.

50. Knedler, 320, n. 15.

51. On this point, see Fenster, 53.

52. See for example, Rose Maria Rosenkötter, "Das Märchen—eine vorwissenschaftliche Entwicklungspsychologie," *Psyche* 34 (1980): 168–207; or Clarice J. Kestenbaum, "Fathers and Daughters: The Father's Contribution to Feminine Identification in Girls as Depicted in Fairy Tales and Myths," *American Journal of Psychoanalysis* 43 (1983): 119–127. One of the few attempts to analyze AT 706 as an Electral projection is Renate Meyer zur Capellen's insightful essay, "Das schöne Mädchen: Psychoanalytische Betrachtungen zur "Formwerdung der Seele' des Mädchens," in Helmut Brackert, ed., *Und wenn sie nicht gestorben sind . . . Perspektiven auf das Märchen* (Frankfurt am Main: Suhrkamp Verlag, 1980) 89–119. However, the author, following the lead provided by Otto Rank's brief analysis of the tale, unfortunately restricts the discussion to the Grimm version alone.

53. Jennifer Waelti-Walters, "On Princesses: Fairy Tales, Sex Roles and Loss of Self," *International Journal of Women's Studies* 2 (1979): 180–188. The quotation is from p. 183. The essay forms the basis of the first chapter of the same author's *Fairy Tales and the Female Imagination* (Montreal: Eden Press, 1982) 1–12.

54. Gary Alan Fine, "Evaluating Psychoanalytic Folklore: Are Freudians Ever Right?" *New York Folklore* 10 (1984): 5–20. For an earlier Freudian reading of "Maiden Without Hands" as a daughter's masturbation fantasy involving her father, see Géza Róheim, "Masturbation Fantasies," *Psychiatric Quarterly* 20 (1946): 661–662.

The Building of Skadar:
The Measure of Meaning
of a Ballad of the Balkans

One of the great collectors of folklore of the nineteenth century was Vuk Karadžić (1787–1864), who almost singlehandedly initiated the serious study of Serbian oral tradition. Like the equally indefatigable folklore collector Evald Tang Kristensen (1843–1929) of Jutland,[1] Karadžić was of humble peasant origin himself and this gave him a lifelong advantage over so-called intellectuals with respect to his being able to understand the nuances of the dialects in which the proverbs, folktales, and folksongs were performed. No theorist, he did amass superb data which inspired other scholars more concerned with theory, notably Jacob Grimm. The details of his difficult but fascinating life are available to an English-reading audience.[2]

It is likely that just as the Grimm brothers may have been impelled to collect German folklore in response to being dominated politically by French culture and rule, so Karadžić's efforts may have been similarly motivated to show the world that Serbian tradition was worthy of being compared to that of Russia and Germany. This is fairly explicit in Vuk's preface to his first volume of folksongs published in 1814.[3] Like the brothers Grimm, he was equally interested in both language and folklore, publishing a dictionary as well as important collections of folktales and folksongs.[4]

On 2 March 1824, Vuk sent the first two volumes of his new edition of folksongs, *Narodne srpske pjesme*, to Jacob Grimm. By the 28th of the same month, Grimm had already made an unmetrical translation of "Zidanje Skadra," "The Building of Skadar," a folksong that greatly impressed him.[5] By May 8th, Grimm had managed a metrical translation of this ballad and he sent it on to Goethe.

The ballad is found throughout the Balkans, where it is known under different titles in different countries. In Greece, it is "The Bridge of Arta," while in Romania, it is often entitled "The Ballad of Master Manole and the Monastery of Argeş." The story is also told in legend form. The ballad or legend plot invariably involves an attempt by a group of masons to construct a castle, bridge, or monastery. Because of some supernatural curse, whatever the builders manage to erect during the day is magically undone at night. By means of either a dream or advice from a spirit—in the Serbian version the spirit is a "vila"[6]—the builders or head mason learn that the spell can be broken only if the first woman (sister, wife) to arrive next day to bring the workers food is walled up in the foundation. The masons (often brothers) agree not to inform their wives so that the unfortunate victim-to-be may be selected by fate or chance. However, all of the brothers except one (e.g., the youngest, or the head mason) fail to honor their covenant. The sad result is that the dutiful wife of the only mason to keep his word comes toward the construction site bearing food for her husband. In some versions, e.g., Romanian, the grief-stricken husband prays to God for a miracle to stop his beloved young wife's progress. But neither lightning nor thunderstorms can prevent the faithful, devoted wife from bringing her husband his meal.

Arriving at the site, the wife is told that as a game or joke, she is to be immured. In some versions (Bulgarian, Greek) she is duped into entering the partly constructed wall by the husband's throwing his wedding ring down into the enclosure and then requesting that she recover it. It is a truly poignant moment in the ballad when the wife comes to the realization that it is no joke or game, and that she is being walled-up forever. In the Romanian version studied by Mircea Eliade, the young bride is pregnant and she cries plaintively, "Manole, Manole, Master Manole, the wall presses me too hard and crushes my breasts and breaks my child."[7] In some versions, including that of Vuk Karadžić, she begs the masons to leave a small aperture, "a window at her breasts," so that she may suckle her infant son.

It is simply not possible to convey the eloquence and emotion of this tragic story with a mere synopsis of the plot. Whether in spoken legend form or as sung as a ballad, the plot has a powerful effect upon all who hear it performed. It is not difficult to document the extraordinary popularity of this ballad throughout the Balkans. In his thorough 1967 survey, Hungarian ballad scholar Lajos Vargyas cites 40 Hungarian, 87 Bulgarian, 49 Romanian, 37 Serbo-Croatian, 14 Albanian, and 297 Greek versions.[8] The ballad has proved to be almost as popular among folklorists as among the folk. I suspect there is probably no ballad among all the many ballads of the world which has been the subject of more articles and monographs than "The Building of Skadar."

Most of the heated debate among Balkans folklorists has centered upon the possible national origin of the ballad. The critical question is inevitably, whose ballad is it really? Typically, the nationality of the writer of the treatise turns out to be the nationality proposed for the *urform* of the ballad. Just as nationalism was a vital force, largely responsible for instigating folklore-collecting activities at the beginning of the nineteenth century, so nationalism continues to be a factor in the scholarly discussions of putative "origins" of individual items of folklore.

Because Vuk Karadžić was the first to collect and publish this ballad, his version has received special prominence. In Vargyas's words, "It was only the great respect accorded to Vuk's variant and his entire collection which led people to regard this variant as a prototype of the whole group of ballads about the walled-up wife. This was the first known variant!"[9]

It would serve little purpose to review the two dozen or more articles and monographs devoted to this ballad, but let me give just a representative sampling of the abundant scholarship to support my assertion that "The Building of Skadar" is the most studied ballad in the history of folkloristics. The relevant references include: Johann K. Schuller, *Kloster Argische, eine romänische Volkssage* (Hermannstadt, 1858); Reinhold Köhler, "Eingemauerte Menschen," *Aufsätze über Märchen und Volkslieder* (Berlin, 1894), 36–47 (first published in 1873); Kurt Schladenbach, "Die aromunische Ballade von der Artabrücke," *Jahresbericht des Instituts für rumanische Sprache* 1 (1894): 79–121; Lazăr Sainean, "Legenda meşterului Manole la Grecii moderni," in *Studii folklorice* (Bucharest, 1896); L. Sainean, "Les rites de construction d'apres la poesie populaire de l'Europe Orientale," *Revue de l'Histoire des Religions* 45 (1902): 359–96; K. Dieterich, "Die Volksdichtung der Balkanländer in ihren gemeinsamen Elementen. Ein Beitrag zur vergleichended Volkskunde I. Die Stoffe," *Zeitschrift für Volkskunde* 12 (1902): 150–52; J. Popovici, "Balada Meşterului Manole," *Rev. Transilvania* (1909): 5–19; M. Arnaudov, "Văgradena nevěsta," [The walled-up young wife] *Sbornik za narodni umotvorenija i narodopis* 34 (Sofia, 1920): 247–528; B. J. Gilliat-Smith, "The Song of the Bridge" (with a note by W. R. Halliday), *Journal of the Gypsy Lore Society*, 3rd Series, 4 (1925): 103–14; Svetislav Stevanovič, *Legenda o zidanju Skadra* (Belgrade, 1928). Petar Skok, "Iz balkanske komparativne literatura. Rumunske paralele 'Zidanju Skadra'," *Glasnik Skopskog naučnog društva* (Skopje, 1929), 220–42; D. Găzdaru, "Legenda Meşterului Manole," *Arhiva* (Taşi, 1932): 88–92; Svetislav Stefanovič, "Die Legende vom Bau der Burg Skutari (Ein Beitrag zur interbalkanische und vergleichenden Sagenforschung)," *Revue Internationale des Études Balkaniques* 1 (1934): 188–210; P. Caraman, "Consideratii critice asupra genezii şi răspândirii baladei Meşterului Manole in Balcani," *Buletinul Institutului de filologie română 'Alexandru Philippide'* 1 (Iaşi, 1934): 62–102; Giuseppe Morici, "La vittima dell'edifizio," *Annali del R. Istituto superiore orientale di Napoli* 9 (1937): 177–216; D. Caracostea, "Material sud-est european şi formă românească," *Revista Fundatiilor regale* (1942): 619–66; Mircea Eliade, *Comentarii la Legenda Meşterului Manole* (Bucharest, 1943); Giuseppe Cocchiara, "Il ponte di Arta. I sacrifici nella letteratura popolare e nella storia del pensiero magico-religioso," *Annali del Museo Pitrè* 1 (1950): 38–81; Ion Taloş, "Balada meşterului Manole şi variantele ei Transilvănene," *Revista de Folclor* 7 (1962): 22–56; Samuel G. Armistead and Joseph H. Silverman, "A Judeo-Spanish Derivative of the Ballad of 'The Bridge of Arta'," *Journal of American Folklore* 76 (1963): 16–20; Mihai Pop, "Nouvelles variantes roumaines du chant du maître Manole," *Romanoslavica* 9 (1963): 427–45; G. Vrabie, *Balada Populare Romana* (Bucharest, 1966), 66–107; Adrien Fochi, "Versiuni extrabalcanice ale legendei despre jertfa zidirii," *Limba si Literatura* 12 (1966), 374–418: Lajos Vargyas,

Researches into the Mediaeval History of Folk Ballad (Budapest, 1967), 173–233; Lorenzo Renzi, *Canti tradizionali romeni* (Florence, 1969), 75–86; Ion Taloş, "Bausagen in Rumänien," *Fabula* 10 (1969): 196–211; Georgios A. Megas, "Die Ballade von der Artas-Brücke," *Zeitschrift für Balkanologie* 7 (1969–70): 43–54; G. Megas, "Tó tragoũdi toũ Gefurioũ tes Artas," *Laografia* 27 (1971): 25–212; Mircea Eliade, "Master Manole and the Monastery of Argeş," in *Zalmoxis: The Vanishing God* (Chicago, 1972), 164–90 (first published in 1955); Grégoire Filiti, "Hypothèse historique sur la genèse de la ballade de Maître Manole," *Südost-Forschungen* 31 (1972): 302–18; Donna Shai, "A Kurdish Jewish Variant of the Ballad of 'The Bridge of Arta'," *AJSreview* 1 (1976): 303–10; Georgios A. Megas, *Die Ballade von der Arta-Brücke: Eine vergleichende Untersuchung* (Thessaloniki: Institute for Balkan Studies, 1976); Zora Devrnja Zimmerman, "Moral Vision in the Serbian Folk Epic: The Foundation Sacrifice of Skadar," *Slavic and East European Journal* 23 (1979): 371–80; Lajos Vargyas, *Hungarian Ballads and the European Ballad Tradition*, vol. 2 (Budapest, 1983), 18–57; Ruth Mandel, "Sacrifice at the Bridge of Arta: Sex Roles and the Manipulation of Power," *Journal of Modern Greek Studies* 1 (1983): 173–83; Eric Tappe, "A Rumanian Ballad and its English Adaptation," *Folklore* 95 (1984): 113–19; Lyubomira Parpulova, "The Ballad of the Walled-Up Wife: Notes about its Structure and Semantics," *Balkan Studies* 25 (1984): 425–39; Zihni Sako, "The Albanian Entombment Ballad and the Other Common Balkan Different Versions," in *Questions of the Albanian Folklore* (Tirana, 1984), 155–65 (first published in 1966); and Zora Devrnja Zimmerman, "The Building of Skadar" and "Commentary," in *Serbian Folk Poetry: Ancient Legends, Romantic Songs* (Columbus, Ohio, 1986), 277–305.[10]

Few scholars possess either the necessary library research resources or the polyglot expertise required to read all that has been written about this unusual ballad. Vargyas, for example, who has himself written probably the best overall survey of the voluminous scholarship devoted to "The Building of Skadar" unaccountably fails to refer to Eliade's 144-page book and his later essay on the subject. But what is even more astonishing, in my opinion, is that with all the monographs and articles written about the ballad, virtually none has plumbed the depths of the ballad's probable meaning and significance.

Most of the discussions of the ballad consist of veritable wars of words seeking to establish the true country or rather nationality of origin. So the ballad, first collected by Karadžić as part of an incipient nationalistic movement to celebrate Serbian culture, has proved to be a scholarly bone of contention between major folklorists of the Balkans. In other words, for more than one hundred years, nationalistic concerns have dominated folkloristic consideration of the ballad. While it is true that the existence of the ballad throughout the Balkans may be said to have greatly encouraged the comparative method, a method predicated upon internationalism rather than nationalism, the published record shows that nearly always the comparative method was employed to demonstrate that the ancestral home of the ballad was the same as the nationality of the writer of the particular discussion. So in typical fashion Greek folklorist Megas concludes one of his essays with the hope that his investigation has made clear "dass Griechenland als Wiege und Heimat unserer Ballade gelten muss." Similarly, Albanian scholar Sako ends his essay with ". . . it seems to us that the original source of the ballad is Illyria, that is, Albania."[11]

Perhaps the first folklorist outside of Yugoslavia to offer any substantial comment on the ballad was Jacob Grimm. He thought it was a magnificent ballad, calling it "einen der rührendsten Gesänge aller Völker und Zeiten," high praise indeed! As mentioned earlier, Grimm sent his translation of the ballad to Goethe who, however, was absolutely horrified by what he considered to be the ballad's gruesome content. In his letter to Jacob Grimm of 30 August 1824 acknowledging receipt of the ballad, Goethe complained of its highly barbaric-heathen sense of human sacrifice.[12] Later, in his review essay on Serbian folksong, Goethe reiterated his distaste by again commenting upon the ballad's reference to human sacrifice of the most disgusting sort. Koljević, in *The Epic in the Making*, remarks that Goethe's attitude is still to be found among modern scholars who continue to feel that "The Building of Skadar" is "an example of savagery" in epic poetry.[13] Koljević condemns this attitude, noting that there is no reason to misread the pathos of the mason-hero's honesty, his wife's suffering, and the grand irony of human goodness "displayed in the little window which Rade the Mason leaves to the victim as he walls her up alive."[14]

The only folklore theory which has been applied to "The Building of Skadar" with any consistency is that of "myth-ritual." According to this nineteenth-century theory, all myth (and other narrative forms directly or indirectly) are assumed to be derived from some earlier type of ritual. The ritual is typically said to be one of fertility, e.g., to ensure a successful agricultural harvest. One serious difficulty with myth-ritual theory is that rarely, if ever, is the origin of the supposed generating ritual explained. To rephrase the critical issue in question, if myth comes from ritual, where does ritual come from? So myth-ritual theory does not offer ultimate origins, merely earlier ritual ones.[15]

In the case of "The Building of Skadar," it did not take long for folklorists to postulate an origin of the ballad in construction rituals. Specifically, it was believed that the ballad arose from the idea of a foundation sacrifice, assumed to be necessary to placate the spirit of the river to be spanned by the bridge-to-be, or the spirit of the ground where a building was to be built. Certainly the plot of "The Building of Skadar" seemed to depend upon the premise that the construction could not succeed without the sacrifice of a human life. From Köhler in 1873 to Sainean in 1902 to Cocchiara in 1950 to Eliade in 1955 to Zimmerman in 1979, this has been the conventional wisdom with respect to interpreting the ballad. Dragutin Subotić in his *Yugoslav Popular Ballads: Their Origin and Development* (Cambridge, 1932), for example, makes the unequivocal statement: "It no doubt goes back to the heathen times when primitive people believed that the Gods in their jealousy allowed men to build strongholds only in return for the sacrifice of human beings."[16] As Koljević noted in 1980, "It is, of course, true that this poem is based on the ancient belief that a human being has to be walled up alive into the foundations of a great edifice if it is to prosper—a belief which can be found not only in Albanian, Macedonian, Bulgarian and Greek variants of this poem, but is also reflected in the Old Testament."[17]

One of the very few critics to object to the construction ritual interpretation of "The Building of Skadar" is the Reverend

Krstivoj Kotur who in his 1977 *The Serbian Folk Epic: Its Theology and Anthropology* proposes a dogmatic Christian interpretation of the ballad as an alternative. Says Kotur, "We cannot accept the opinion of some native as well as foreign interpreters of Serbian folk poetry who see in the poem "The Erection of Skutari" a remnant of the old heathen thoughts of sacrifice to the "heathen gods" without which men would be punished for attempting to build something."[18] Instead, argues Kotur, the poet arranges that an innocent creature is entombed, "an innocent being suffers for the sins of others. This is the message of the poem."[19] The sins of the family involved are "entirely too large for them to be redeemed thereof through a personal sacrifice or the price of one of them. Therefore, a higher sacrifice—that of an innocent person—is necessary. Is this not a complete analogy with the redemption of the sinful human race by the Son of God? . . . In its Christian reflection of the poem now lies its value, and simultaneously, the greatness of the folk poet."[20] In this way, Kotur concludes, the poem does not involve a heathenish motif of human sacrifice, but rather the pure Christian principle of the redemption of sin through the sacrifice of an innocent. Needless to say, there are very few legitimate Serbian scholars who would subscribe to this partisan Christian reading of "The Building of Skadar."[21]

The principal problem with the myth-ritual (and for that matter, the Christian) reading of the ballad is that it utterly fails to explain nearly all the specific details of the ballad. Why, for example, must it be a *woman* who is the human sacrifice? Surely myth-ritual theory would be equally well served no matter who or what the victim was. What of the agreement among the builders not to tell their wives, an agreement honored only by the one male builder whose wife is victimized? What has that to do with myth-ritual theory and the notion of foundation sacrifice? How does myth-ritual theory explain the curious, but oft-repeated detail of the husband dropping his wedding ring into the construction wall? It should be perfectly obvious that the construction sacrifice ritual even if it is valid—and there is not a single shred of evidence that the ballad or legend was ever sung or recited in connection with an actual construction ritual—is not sufficient to explain all the remarkable nuances of so dramatic a plot. No theory in folkloristics can be deemed adequate unless or until it makes it possible to understand *all* the details of an item of folklore.

One of the most serious criticisms of the application of myth-ritual theory to "The Building of Skadar" is that it reflects a totally *literal* approach to the ballad. Literal or purely historical approaches to folklore data are inevitably doomed to failure insofar as folklore contains fantasy. To the extent that folklore consists of fiction, not fact, fantasy, not reality, an exclusively literal-minded approach cannot possibly succeed in elucidating the totality of folklore content. In folklore proper, it is only fools who insist upon interpreting metaphors literally (cf. the section of the *Motif-Index* dealing with J2450–J2499 Literal fools).[22] Zimmerman, for example, suggests that the ballad be understood as a metaphor, but she insists upon interpreting the metaphor literally: "'The Building of Skadar' is based on a metaphorical equation: 'the foundation of a city is the mother of a city' . . . To immure a nursing mother insures the strength of the foundations, especially while the mother's milk is flowing."[23] For Zimmerman, bogged down in the myth-ritual approach, the ballad may have arisen from "Guilt-ridden cultural memories about foundation sacrifices."[24]

With respect to "The Building of Skadar," I submit it is time to put aside the highly emotional issues of nationalism—it does not really matter whether the ballad originated in Albania, Bulgaria, Greece, Hungary, Yugoslavia, or elsewhere. It is enough to note that the ballad is extremely popular in all of these countries. For that matter, if ever the origin of the ballad is definitively determined, that discovery will have to take account of cognate versions of the story from India, versions hitherto ignored by Balkanologists.

In Central India among the Santals we find a tale in which there are seven brothers and a sister. The brothers try to dig a well but are unable to find water. A passing Yogi advises the brothers to sacrifice their sister (who is about to married) if they wish to secure water. The brothers except for the youngest agree to do so. They tell their mother to have the sister "dressed in her best" when she "brought them out their midday meal" next day. When she arrives, the brothers ask her to draw water from the dry tank/well. When she reaches the area, water begins to bubble up from

the earth. It rises to her instep. However, each time she attempts
to fill her container, it will not fill—even as the water continues
to rise higher and higher. The girl proceeds to sing a series of
verses clearly analogous to those sung by the corresponding victim
in the Balkans ballad:

> The water has risen, brother,
> And wetted my ankle, brother,
> But still the *lota* in my hand
> Will not sink below the surface.

In succession, the water wets her knees, waist, and neck. Finally,
the water covers her head, drowning her, but at that point the *lota*
or water-pot is filled.

The Indic tales, unlike most of the Balkans ballads, do not stop
at this point. The innocent girl does not die, but is transformed
or reincarnated into the form of a flower or fiddle. Later the girl
is reconstituted and marries. Eventually the brothers' treachery is
revealed and they are appropriately punished, e.g., by being swal-
lowed up by a chasm caused by a sudden split in the earth.[25]

Just as nationalistic debate about the origins of the ballad might
be usefully suspended, so also it is time to escape from the overly
rigid literal mindset which has insisted for one hundred years that
the ballad concerns a ritual sacrifice. Let us assume for the sake
of argument that the ballad has nothing whatever to do with foundation sacrifice. What then is the ballad really about?

I suggest that the ballad is an exquisite metaphorical expression
of woman's role in the Balkans. The initial premise demonstrates
the standard division of labor whereby men work *outside* of the
home while women remain *inside* at home. In the ballad, women
are evidently permitted to leave the house in order to serve men,
e.g., bring them their lunch. More specifically, I believe the ballad
is about marriage in particular which is depicted as having a dire
impact upon women's life expectations. In essence, the women
must be sacrificed for men to do their (men's) work. Marriage,
for a woman, means being locked up for life, that is, until death.
Now we can better understand the bitter irony of the mason's
dropping his wedding ring down into the construction side. The
woman is duped into entering her tomb in pursuit of a wedding

ring! How much more explicit can the metaphor be than that! The only window to the outside world—in some versions of the ballad—is that she may offer her breast to her baby. The welfare of the baby, preferably a son, is the only reason not to immure the young wife completely. Again, it is service to males which provides the only outlet.

The treachery of the other masons in revealing the sacrifice agreement to their wives again refers to the central male-female dichotomy in the Balkans. The poor male who does trust his fellow males discovers that it costs him the life of his young bride. Male mistrust results not in the death of a male, but in the death of a female. It is evidently women who must pay for the crimes of men. Accordingly, in the ballad, a young bride is martyred through no fault or choice of her own. It is rather through the wheelings and dealings of men that she becomes eternally immobilized inside a castle, or bridge or monastery. She becomes, one is tempted to say, a permanent victim of the Balkans' male edifice complex.

In assessing the plausibility and possible validity of this symbolic reading of the ballad "The Building of Skadar," one might legitimately ask to what extent, if any, does the female role delineated correspond to the facts of ethnographic reality? We know that young brides in Serbia lived in their husbands' households and that they had little or no status until they produced offspring, preferably male. The wedding songs commonly employed images of marriage as death. Kligman observes in Romania, for example, that "For a girl, marriage is metaphorically equated with death."[26] Russian folklorist Sokolova claims that the "death-marriage" metaphor recurs in the folklore of almost all Slavonic peoples.[27]

Anthropologist Andrei Simić, a specialist in Yugoslav ethnography, remarks that "the theme of the martyred and self-sacrificing mother appears repeatedly in South Slav epic poetry,"[28] and he specifically cites "The Building of Skadar" as an illustration. But more importantly his fieldwork interviews confirm the contemporary existence of the theme. "A similar stereotyping of mothers in terms of sacredness, devotion, sublime altruism, and martyrdom was frequently expressed by informants.[29] One informant interviewed about the ballad by Zimmerman said, "She always had to cry when she heard this poem. 'It is so terrible, so tragic, How can men be so brutal?' "[30]

That such a sexist view of women may be found in scholarship as well as in folk poetry may be demonstrated by referring to Vladimir Dvorniković's *Karakterologija Jugoslavena* (Belgrade, 1930) in which it is suggested that part of South Slavic national character includes a penchant for passive suffering. There was the famous battle of Kossovo (June 28, 1389) in which the Serbs were defeated by the Turks, but the disaster or defeat was perceived as a form of sacrifice for national honor. As one author words it: "No people in the history of mankind except the Serbs has ever taken pride in a national disaster."[31] But let us observe precisely how Dvorniković discusses this alleged component of Serbian national character. "The Slav is predisposed toward passive suffering. . . . Is there, then, in this boundless capacity for suffering something *feminine*, or is it a sign of the primeval obtuseness and immovability, a sign of the capacity to endure and suffer everything in the manner of a 'dumb animal'?"[32]

We may read the ballad's metaphor in slightly different language: through marriage, a young woman is buried alive inside the construction built by her husband. The slow painful death, only partly alleviated by sometimes being able to nurse her male heir, offers little hope for the Serbian woman. In Vuk Karadžić's version of the ballad, even after the poor young bride dies, her breasts continue to provide milk for her infant. The baby is brought to the immured wife:

> And she suckled it for seven days.
> After seven days her voice was silent,
> But the milk still flowed for the baby,
> And she suckled it for a whole year.
>   Thus it was, and thus it remains,
> Even today the milk will flow there
> For a wonder and for the healing
> Of any woman that has no milk.[33]

The ending confirms the importance of the nurturant role for Serbian women (and also that the welfare of the infant son takes precedence over the very life of the mother). Even in death, the woman must continue to nurture, to serve males food. Recall that the young woman braved rainstorm and lightning in order to bring *food* to her husband on the job. No wonder this ballad is so popular in the Balkans and no wonder so many male folklorists in the Balkans have chosen to study the ballad and to claim it as part of their very own *patri*mony!

It should perhaps be noted that the feminist symbolic reading of "The Building of Skadar" is not necessarily mutually exclusive with the earlier myth-ritual interpretation of the ballad. Both theoretical applications might well apply. Perhaps the ballad did arise originally from an actual ritual custom of human sacrifice, but whether it did or not, it would appear that the interpretation proposed in this essay would at least better explain why the victim has to be a woman and why it makes perfect sense for her to be duped into entering her tomb through pursuit of a wedding ring. If the women of the Balkans wish to cease being buried alive in a world constructed by and for men, there will have to be drastic changes in traditional Balkans social organization and in the standard roles assigned to men and women. In the meantime, the plight of Serbian and other Balkans women is presumably all too well depicted in "The Building of Skadar" and its cognate forms.

What began as a single ballad collected by a great folklorist, Vuk Karadžić, in the first decades of the nineteenth century as part of a nationalistic patriotic movement, and was subjected to an endless succession of petty nationalistic arguments over origins for more than a century, can now be placed in an international framework as a striking metaphorical statement about the life and fate of women, not just in one country, but throughout the Balkans and wherever else the ballad is known.

NOTES

1. For an account of this remarkable folklore collector, see Joan Rockwell, *Evald Tang Kristensen: A Lifelong Adventure in Folklore* (Aalborg: Aalborg University Press, 1982). For an analysis of some of the texts he collected, see Bengt Holbek, *Interpretation of Fairy Tales: Danish Folklore in a European Perspective*, FF Communications No. 239 (Helsinki: Academia Scientiarum Fennica, 1987).

2. The standard source is Duncan Wilson, *The Life and Times of Vuk Stefanović Karadžić (1787–1864)* (Oxford: Clarendon Press, 1970). For an appreciation of his work in folklore, see Yvonne R. Lockwood, "Vuk

Stefanović Karadžić: Pioneer and Continuing Inspiration of Yugoslav Folkloristics," *Western Folklore* 30 (1971): 19–32. See also Alexander M. Trbovich, "Vuk Karadžić," *Slavia* 16 (1941): 183–89, and V. Corović, "Vuk Karadžić," *The Slavonic Review* 16 (1937–38): 667–77.

3. This preface is translated in part as Appendix E in Wilson, op.cit., 395–400. See also 90–94.

4. Cf. Wilson, 195. For a consideration of Vuk's contribution to folktale collection, see Maja Bošković-Stulli, "Die Volksmärchen Vuk Karadžić's als Schätzungsmassstab der Serbokroatischen Märchen," in Georgios A. Megas, ed., *IV International Congress for Folk-Narrative Research in Athens: Lectures and Reports* (Athens, 1965), 27–36.

5. Stjepan Tropsch, "Jakob Grimm als Übersetzer Serbo-Kroatischer Volkslieder," *Euphorion* 16 (1923): 106–20. See 114. For more detail about Grimm's abiding interest in Serbian folklore, see Miljan Mojasević, "Jacob Grimm und die Jugoslawen: Skizze und Stoff zu einer Studie," *Hessische Blätter für Volkskunde* 54 (1963): 333–65.

6. For a brief account of what a *vila* is, see Appendix III in Svetozar Koljević, *The Epic in the Making* (Oxford: Clarendon Press, 1980), 347–48. For more detail, see Zora Devrnja Zimmerman, "The Changing Roles of the *Vila* in Serbian Traditional Literature," *Journal of the Folklore Institute* 16 (1979): 167–75.

7. Mircea Eliade, "Master Manole and the Monastery of Argeş," in *Zalmoxis: The Vanishing God* (Chicago: University of Chicago Press, 1972), 168.

8. Lajos Vargyas, *Researches into the Mediaeval History of Folk Ballad* (Budapest: Akadémiai Kiadó, 1967), 174–77. These figures are not firm. For example, there are at least 330 Greek versions of the ballad. See Vargyas, *Hungarian Ballads and the European Ballad Tradition*, vol. II (Budapest: Akadémiai Kiadó, 1983), 55.

9. Vargyas, *Researches*, 209.

10. This is by no means an exhaustive list. For additional references, see Eliade, 165, n.1; Vargyas, *Researches*, 173–233; and Vargyas, *Hungarian Ballads*, 55–57. See also Paul G. Brewster, "The Foundation Sacrifice Motif in Legend, Folksong, Game, and Dance," *Zeitschrift für Ethnologie* 96 (1971), 71–89.

11. G. Megas, "Die Ballade von der Artas-Brücke," *Zeitschrift für Balkanologie* 7 (1969–70): 54; Z. Sako, "The Albanian Entombment Ballad and the Other Common Balkan Different Versions," in *Questions of the Albanian Folklore* (Tirana: 8 Nentori Publishing House, 1984), 165. Sako's conclusions actually were stated much earlier. See "Elements Balkaniques Communs dans le Rite de la Balade de l'Emmurement," *Studia Albanica*, IIIe Annee, no. 2 (1966): 207–13.

12. Jevto M. Milović, *Goethe, seine Zeitgenossen und die serbokroatische Volkspoesie, Veröffentlichungen des Slavischen Instituts an der Friedrich-Wilhelms-Universität Berlin* (Leipzig, 1941), 51. See also Milan

Curčin, "Goethe and Serbo-Croat Ballad Poetry," *The Slavonic Review* 11 (1932–33): 126–34.

13. Koljević, 150.

14. *Ibid.*

15. For a sample of the rich myth-ritual scholarship, see Theodor H. Gaster, "Myth and Story," in Alan Dundes, ed., *Sacred Narrative: Readings in the Theory of Myth* (Berkeley: University of California Press, 1984), 110–36. See also Robert A. Segal, "The Myth-Ritualist Theory of Religion," *Journal for the Scientific Study of Religion* 19 (1980): 173–85.

16. Dragutin Subotić, *Yugoslav Popular Ballads*, 39.

17. Koljević, 147.

18. Rev. Dr. Krstivoj Kotur, *The Serbian Folk Epic: Its Theology and Anthropology* (New York: Philosophical Library, 1977), 181.

19. Kotur, 184.

20. Kotur, 185.

21. But see Zora Devrnja Zimmerman, "Moral Vision in the Serbian Folk Epic: The Foundation Sacrifice of Skadar," *Slavic and East European Journal* 23 (1979): 371–80. For the notion that the ballad reflects Christian concepts, see 372, 378.

22. Stith Thompson, *Motif-Index of Folk-Literature*, 6 vols. (Bloomington: Indiana University Press, 1955–58). Motifs relevant to the ballad include D 2192 Work of day magically overthrown at night, and S 261 Foundation sacrifice.

23. Zora Devrnja Zimmerman, *Serbian Folk Poetry: Ancient Legends, Romantic Songs* (Columbus, Ohio: Kosovo Publishing Co., 1986), 301.

24. Zimmerman, "Moral Vision in the Serbian Folk Epic," 379.

25. Cecil Henry Bompas, *Folklore of the Santal Parganas* (London: David Nutt, 1909), 102–6. I am indebted to Dr. Ali Ferdowsi for bringing this and other Indic texts to my attention. For other versions from India, see A. Campbell, *Santal Folk Tales* (Pokhuria: Santal Mission Press, 1891), 52–56, 106–10. See also Sarah Davidson and Eleanor Phelps, "Folk Tales from New Goa, India," *Journal of American Folklore* 50 (1937): 47–48. The ballad is enormously popular in south India. For representative Telugu versions, see Rallapalli Gopalakrishna Sarma, "Gangabhavāni-Narabali," *Janapadam* 9 (March 1982): 1–4. (I am indebted to Dr. R.V.S. Sundaram for this reference.) For sample Kannada texts, see Devendrakumāra C. Hakāri, *Janapada Sāmājika Kathanagītagalalli Duhkhānta Nirūpane* (Bangalore: Kannada Sāhitya Parishat, 1985), 247–63. (I thank Professor A.K. Ramanajan for this reference.) The parallels between the Indic and Balkans texts are too extraordinary to be coincidence. In "The Magic Fiddle" (Campbell, 52–53, the sister betrayed by her seven brothers begins to wail: "Oh! my brother, the water reaches to my ankles (knees, waist, breast, neck, etc.), and this sequence is virtually identical to the series in Bulgarian and Hungarian ballads:

knees, waist, breast, head, etc. (cf. Vargyas, *Researches*, 220–21). Also in some Serbian, Albanian and Romanian versions of the ballad, the victim is not the wife, but the sister of the builder. Vargyas, *Researches*, 202, labels this a secondary element. In view of the well locus of the Indic texts, it may be significant that sometimes in the Balkans ballad, the story ends with a well of milk or *water* stemming from the place where the woman was walled up. See Vargyas, *Hungarian Ballads*, 43.

The Indic texts are strongly reminiscent of a well-known folktale, namely, Aarne-Thompson tale type 780, The Singing Bone, in which a brother kills his brother or sister. From the bones, a harp or flute is made which reveals the murder. See Antti Aarne and Stith Thompson, *The Types of the Folktale*, FF Communications No. 184 (Helsinki: Academia Scientiarum Fennica, 1961). If, and this is only a hypothesis, the Indic texts of A-T 780 proved to be the ancestral form from which the Balkans ballad ultimately derived, then the ballad would have to be understood as a truncated variant of the folktale. The reason why peoples of the Balkans chose to have their version of the story end with tragedy rather than with the resuscitation of the victim and the punishment of the brothers might be related to Balkans worldview. The possible connection between local versions of the ballad and differing worldviews is supported by a hitherto unnoticed distinctive feature of most of the south Indian texts. In Kannada versions, for example, the female to be sacrificed *knows in advance* that her death is required in order for the water tank to be filled. Usually she overhears a conversation and then she typically visits her parents to say a sad goodbye to them. Unlike the Balkans versions where the female is invariably duped (by males) into becoming a sacrificial victim, the Indic texts involve the equally poignant issue of self-sacrifice. The Indic female knowingly goes to her death, ostensibly for the welfare of her husband or the community, an action entirely consonant with a culture in which suttee was once the convention.

26. Gail Kligman, "The Rites of Women: Oral Poetry, Ideology, and the Socialization of Peasant Women in Contemporary Romania," *Journal of American Folklore* 97 (1984): 186, n.8. See also I. Muslea, "La mort mariage: une particularité du folklore balcanique," *Cercetări Etnografice şi de Folclor* (Bucharest, 1972), 7–36, and Gail Kligman, *The Wedding of the Dead: Ritual, Poetics, and Popular Culture in Transylvania* (Berkeley: University of California Press, 1988), 218–20. Some interpreters of the ballad assume the subject is literal, not metaphorical death. Roderick Beaton, for example, suggests "The Bridge of Arta" is, at least in Greek tradition, "connected in some way with myths concerning the passage from life to death." See his *Folk Poetry of Modern Greece* (Cambridge: Cambridge University Press, 1980), 123, 128.

27. V.K. Sokolova, "Some Traditional Symbols in Slavonic Folk Poetry," in Alan Dundes, ed., *Varia Folklorica* (The Hague: Mouton, 1978), 155–63. See especially 160.

28. Andrei Simić, "Machismo and Cryptomatriarchy: Power, Affect, and Authority in the Contemporary Yugoslav Family," *Ethos* 11 (1983): 66–86. The quotation appears on 80.

29. Simić, 81. Jovan Brkić in his *Moral Concepts in Traditional Serbian Epic Poetry* (The Hague: Mouton, 1961), 74, observes that "It was considered a sin if the wife acted against her husband, even though the circumstances might have warranted it." Others have commented upon the subservient status of Serbian wives. Bette S. Denich in "Sex and Power in the Balkans," in Michelle Zimbalist Rosaldo and Louise Lamphere, eds., *Woman, Culture, and Society* (Stanford: Stanford University Press, 1974), 251, remarks "Only as the mother of sons does a wife secure a place in the group, bound to it through a blood tie."

30. Zimmerman, *Serbian Folk Poetry*, 295.

31. Kotur, *The Serbian Folk Epic*, 131–32.

32. Dvorniković, as cited in Kotur, 144, emphasis added.

33. Wilson, 372. I should indicate that Ruth Mandel in her essay "Sacrifice at the Bridge of Arta: Sex Roles and the Manipulation of Power," *Journal of Modern Greek Studies* 1 (1983): 173–83, does employ a symbolic approach to the ballad. However, she elects to concentrate upon women's liminal status—between insider and outsider. She suggests (180) that male culture lacks the creativity "inherent in female nature and therefore must take it from the woman. Culture appropriates nature." Man conquers nature, according to Mandel, by spanning the river and destroying woman-as-nature. While the bridge could itself be liminal—linking two sides of a river, the reading might not be quite so applicable to other versions of the ballad where a castle rather than a bridge is the object under construction.

Another intriguing interpretation of the ballad clearly sympathetic to a feminist perspective is Parpulova's suggestion that underlying both the ballad and the "construction code" is a series of rites of passage related to "marriage and the delivery of the first child." However, Parpulova is unfortunately unable to escape the restrictive vise of myth-ritual theory. She argues for the possibility that there is "a myth lying at the root of both the rite and the ballad," and further suggests that actual ritual separation customs (separating the new mother from society for some period after childbirth) may have given rise to the theme of the walled-up wife-mother. See Lyubomira Parpulova, "The Ballad of the Walled-Up Wife," *Balkan Studies* 25 (1984): 427, 435, 436.

Another example of an obviously limited interpretation of the ballad is Zimmerman's suggestion that "The immurement, in this context, can represent the subjugation of the Serbian peoples at the time, and the survival of the infant, the ultimate survival of the nation." See Zimmerman, "Moral Vision in the Serbian Folk Epic," 379. This interpretation would scarcely apply to all the versions of the ballad found in other countries. The point is that local nationalistic interpretations of international ballads may not be sufficient to explain the underlying content and significance of such ballads. While it is perfectly possible that the "same" ballad might be interpreted differently in different cultural contexts, it is equally possible that a given ballad might be relevant to a variety of cultures or nations for more or less the same reason. Certainly the interpretation proposed in this essay is intended to apply to virtually all the versions of the ballad reported. Even in the Santal text from India, the victim is about to be married and she comes to the well "Dressed in her best" (as if for a wedding?). The gradual "covering" of the body by the water or wall does tend to emphasize the female body parts in succession thereby "dis" covering them. In these cultures, a woman is expected to sacrifice her body and life for her husband. Accordingly, marriage literally and figuratively seals the fate of young brides. Marriage means immobility and confinement until death.

Index

Aarne, Antti, 66, 69, 72, 118
Abraham, Karl, 120, 137
adhesions, 61
Afanasyev, A. N., 74, 114, 115, 123
age-area hypothesis, 64
Aladdin folktale, 145
apple symbolism, 128–29, 131
April Fish, 99–102, 108
April Fool, 98–111
Aquinas, Thomas, 3
Arnim, Achim von, 117

Balinese cockfight, 63, 73
Barth, Frederik, 14
Basques, 6, 15–16
Bauman, Richard, 8
Beidelman, Tom, 63
Bettelheim, Bruno, 121
Boas, Franz, 59, 60–61, 63, 67
Bolte, Johannes, 65, 133
book-keepers, 1
Botkin, Benjamin, 41, 50
Brentano, Clemens, 117
Bunyan, Paul, 40–41, 47, 49, 50, 53

Calame-Griaule, Genevieve, 130–31
Calm before the storm, 95
cartographic method, 72
catches, 16–17

charivari, 98, 105–6, 109
Chaucer, Geoffrey, 118
Cinderella, 22, 34, 44, 70, 130, 132–33, 139
comparative method, 57–82, 87
computer joke, 35
contrada, 14–15
Coote, Henry Charles, 135–36
couvade, 62
Cox, Marian R., 132–33, 138
cradles, 21
Crane, Thomas F., 69
cultural relativism, 71, 73n, 74

dainas, 9–10
De Coster, Charles, 52
Dedalus, Stephen, 1
Delta Chi fraternity, 30–31
DeVos, George, 8, 9
Dorson, Richard M., 40–41, 57, 50, 52
dream origin of fairy tales, 126–27
Dvorniković, Vladimir, 162

earth resting on a turtle's back, 75
Eggan, Fred, 61
Electra complex, 127, 138, 142
Eliade, Mircea, 152, 155, 157
Ellison, Ralph, 25
Erikson, Erik, 5, 7, 9, 12, 26, 83
ethnicity, 11
Eulenspiegel, 52

fakelore, 40–56, 118, 145
finger ring, symbolism of, 114–15, 139
Finnish Literature Society, 45
Finnish method, 60, 64, 65, 66, 67, 68, 73, 74, 125
fixed phrase genres, 93
flyleaf inscriptions, 1–2, 12
folk, concept of, 10, 11
folk art, 84
folk museums, 50
folklorismus, 53
food supply, 85, 86, 89
fool's errand, 98–100, 105, 107
forbidden chamber, 128
Foster, Stephen, 26
Frau Holle folktale, 121, 125–31
Frazer, James George, 58, 74, 136
free phrase genres, 93
Freud, Sigmund, 7, 112–13, 114, 115, 116, 117, 120, 143
frog prince folktale, 125
fur symbolism, 140

Galton, Francis, 62
games, 18–19
Geertz, Clifford, 63
giants, psychoanalytic theory of, 124–25
Gibbon, Edward, 48
glass slipper, 139–40
glottochronology, 76
Goethe, J. W. von, 49, 152, 156
gowk, 99
goyim, 28
Grimm, Jacob, 44, 66, 151, 156
Grimm, Wilhelm, 44, 117
Grimm brothers, 44–45, 52, 64, 100, 112–50
Grundtvig, Svend, 66
Gubernatis, Angelo de, 102, 135

Haavio, Martti, 46
Halloween, 20, 98, 108, 109

Hansel and Gretel folktale, 121, 125
Heraclitus, 3
Herder, J. G. von, 9, 118
Herodotus, 58
historic-geographic method, 64, 65; see also comparative method
historical reconstruction of the past, 64
homosexual dress code, 31–32
Honko, Lauri, 65–66
Honti, Hans, 70, 126
Huckleberry Finn, 17
Human Relations Area Files, 62
human sacrifice, 156, 158
Hume, David, 1, 4, 42, 48

Identity, 1–39, 70
infantocentric perspective, 125
inferiority feelings, 51
instant identity, 32
Invisible Man, 25

Jack and the Beanstalk folktale, 128
Jason, Heda, 71
John Henry, 26–27
Joyce, James, 1
Jung, C. G., 59

Kaguru folktale, 63, 73
Kalevala, 45–47, 53, 65
Karadžić, Vuk, 151, 152, 153, 156, 162, 163
Kinder- und Hausmärchen, 42, 44, 45, 53, 124
King Lear, 133
Kligman, Gail, 161
Koljević, Svetozar, 156, 157
Kotur, Krstivoj, 158
Krappe, Alexander H., 136–37
Kristensen, Evald Tang, 151
Krohn, Julius, 65, 66
Krohn, Kaarle, 46, 64–65, 66, 70, 71, 72, 118

Lafitau, Joseph-François, 58
Lang, Andrew, 58–59
laws of culture, 71
lecherous father motif, 132, 140
Lévi-Strauss, Claude, 3, 105, 109, 122
Lévy-Bruhl, Lucien, 59
lex talionis, 141
Lightning never strikes twice, 94
Linton, Ralph, 14
literal vs. metaphorical interpretation, 94–95, 127, 128, 139, 140, 144, 159, 160, 166
literalization of metaphor as basis of magic, 94
Little Red Riding Hood folktale, 70, 112, 121
Locke, John, 4–5
Lönnrot, Elias, 45–46, 47
Lüthi, Max, 121
Lunding, Astrid, 66

M.O.T., 30
Macpherson, James, 42–43, 47, 48
magic, principles of, 74
magpies, 95, 97
Maiden Without Hands folktale, 131–42
Mallet, Carl-Heinz, 121
marriage-death equation, 161
masturbation, 130, 141, 145, 150
Mead, Margaret, 6, 28
medical school student prank, 103–4
Megas, Georgios, 156
Merchant of Venice, 113
Mieder, Wolfgang, 92
monogenesis, 60, 71, 86
Müller, Max, 66, 135
multi-group slur, 23–24
multiple existence and variation, 85
myth-ritual theory, 126, 157, 163, 167

name change joke, 27–28
national character, 22, 73
national stereotype, 22–24
nature mythology, 125, 135
number jokes, 34
numbers, 33–34

Oedipus, 19, 21–22, 122, 138
oicotype, 72–73, 85, 87
Olrik, Axel, 65, 72
One swallow does not make a summer, 95
Oppenheim, D. E., 113–16
Ossian, 42–43, 47, 48, 50 53
oven symbolism, 125, 128, 146

pecking chicken toy, 83–91
personal space, 85, 89
Pitrè, Giuseppe, 100, 115
Poggio, 114, 115
Polívka, Georg, 134
polygenesis, 60, 71, 86
pranks, 98–111
primitive mentality, 59
projective inversion, 28–29, 138, 140, 142
Propp, Vladimir, 21, 74, 122, 123, 127, 130, 142–43
proverbs, 4, 92–97
puberty rites, 127, 130–31

Randolph, Vance, 117
Rank, Otto, 138, 141
Red sky at night, 93
reductionism, 123
Reichard, Gladys, 67–68, 69
revival, 41
Richmond, W. Edson, 31
riddles, 19–20
Riklin, Franz, 138
rites of passage, 106–7
ritual reversal of seasons, 109
Roberts, Warren, 121, 125, 129
Róheim, Géza, 113, 121, 126–27

Sako, Zihni, 156
same-sex opposition in folktales, 124
Scherf, Walter, 121
Schlauch, Margaret, 136
Search for the Lost Husband folktale, 130
self-fulfilling prophecy, 24
self-hate, 24–25
sexual identity, 16–17
Shakespeare, William, 113, 133
shoe symbolism, 138–39, 149
shvartzer, 29–30
Siena, 14–15
Simić, Andrei, 161
Skadar, the Building of, 151–68
snipe hunt, 105
Snow White, 25–26
Sokolova, Vera, 161
solar mythology, 126
source criticism, 62
Spicer, Edward H., 7–8, 9
Star Husband folktale, 67–68
Stefanović, Svetislav, 136
sub-type, 73, 85
superorganic, 71–72
superstition, 92–97
survival, 41
suttee, 166

Table, ass, and stick folktale, 120
tale type, concept of, 70–71, 112
Tallman, Richard S., 102–3
Taylor, Archer, 66, 67, 92, 137

Tell, William, 52
Thompson, Stith, 67, 68, 69, 118, 135
toilet training, 74
trickster, 25
Twain, Mark, 17
Tylor, Edward B., 58, 59, 61–62

unilinear evolutionary theory, 58, 59, 136
ur-form, 64, 72, 153

vagina dentata motif, explanation of, 147
van Gennep, Arnold, 74, 106
Vargyas, Lajos, 153, 155
von Sydow, Carl Wilhelm, 65, 67

weather "proverbs," 92–97
Weber, Max, 8
wedding ring thrown into enclosure, 152, 158, 160–61, 163
wedding symbolism, 114
well symbolism, 127–28
Westermarck, Edward, 59
Wilder, Thornton, 2
Wilson, William, 46, 49
Winterstein, A., 127
wishful thinking, 18, 26, 127, 137, 142
world-view, 83, 87, 89, 90

Zimmerman, Zora D., 159, 161